T

CHRISTIAN
WORLD
of
THE
HOBBIT

DEVIN BROWN

Abingdon Press
NASHVILLE

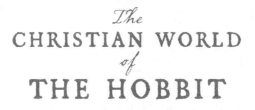

The
CHRISTIAN WORLD
of
THE HOBBIT

This book is printed on acid-free paper.

Library of Congress Cataloging-in-Publication Data has been requested.

ISBN 978-1-4267-4949-0

12 13 14 15 16 17 18 19 20 21—10 9 8 7 6 5 4 3 2 1

MANUFACTURED IN THE UNITED STATES OF AMERICA

Praise for *The Christian World of The Hobbit*

The title of Devin Brown's new book is sure to raise some eyebrows. How could a world filled with dwarves, elves, goblins, wizards, and hobbits be considered "Christian"? Brown uses what we know about the author of the famous children's story, along with his attention to the details and careful wording of *The Hobbit*, to show how J. R. R. Tolkien wove his faith into its pages.

—Mark Sommer, Fantasy Editor for HollywoodJesus.com

Like Tolkien himself, Devin Brown steals past the watchful dragons of accredited literary culture to explain how Tolkien's works can embody a Christian worldview without preaching or propaganda, and what this has to do with how those stories lift the heart.

—Tom Shippey, Tolkien Scholar

In far too many cases, Tolkien's remarkable novels are taken to extremes by readers. Some pronounce no spiritual elements in the stories, while others find Christian symbolism where there is none. Devin Brown's new book *The Christian World of The Hobbit* brilliantly balances those extremes. Tolkien's Christian faith was a vital part of *The Hobbit*, and I'm thrilled such an accurate book finally tells the real story.

—Phil Cooke, Filmmaker, Media Consultant, and Author of *One Big Thing: Discovering What You Were Born to Do*

To my mother,
who always encouraged me to read

CONTENTS

INTRODUCTION

On October 2, 1937, readers opened the *Times Literary Supplement* to find a review of a remarkable new book.

"This is a children's book only in the sense that the first of many readings can be undertaken in the nursery," the reviewer explained. He also made the point that the book "will be funniest to its youngest readers, and only years later, at a tenth or a twentieth reading, will they begin to realize what deft scholarship and profound reflection have gone to make everything in it so ripe, so friendly, and in its own way so true."

The reviewer was C. S. Lewis. The book was *The Hobbit*. Its author was an obscure Oxford philologist named J. R. R. Tolkien.

Of all the things Lewis said in his review, his closing statement—one that may have seemed quite bold back in

1937—proved to be the most accurate of all. "Prediction is dangerous," Lewis concluded, "but *The Hobbit* may well prove a classic" ("Hobbit," 82).

Lewis's prediction was an understatement, as *The Hobbit* and its sequel, *The Lord of the Rings*, gradually but steadily went on to win the hearts of readers everywhere. As the twentieth century drew to a close, magazine editors, literary critics, and pundits came up with a seemingly endless series of polls, surveys, and top 100 lists. When it came to the best book or best author of the past hundred years, in poll after poll, survey after survey, list after list, J. R. R. Tolkien was always at the top.

At Waterstones, the giant British bookstore, *The Lord of the Rings* was declared the book of the century after it received the most votes at 104 of its 105 branches (the lone exception was a branch where Joyce's *Ulysses* came in first and *The Lord of the Rings* second). When the *Daily Telegraph* asked readers across the United Kingdom to vote for their favorite author and favorite book, Tolkien and *The Lord of the Rings* won again. The members of the Folio Society, also in England, ranked *The Lord of the Rings* first with *Pride and Prejudice* second. Tolkien's epic was at the top of a poll to determine the "Nation's Best-Loved Book" taken by the BBC, and at the top of similar polls in Australia and Germany. Not to be outdone, Amazon.com customers voted *The Lord of the Rings* as the best book of the millennium. In *Christianity Today*'s survey of the Best 100

Religious Books of the Century, J. R. R. Tolkien and *The Lord of the Rings* came in fourth, ahead of works by such notable Christian authors as Richard Foster, Oswald Chambers, and Reinhold Niebuhr. *The Hobbit* was number twenty-five in the BBC's Big Read list of the Top 100 Books. The teachers of the National Education Association placed *The Hobbit* in their list of 100 Best Books.

And in the second decade of the 21st century, sales of Tolkien's books continue to rise, making any statement outdated as soon as it is given. Current estimates place sales of *The Lord of the Rings* at more than 150 million copies and sales of *The Hobbit* at more than 100 million, making them among the best-selling books of all time.

Many explanations have been proposed for Tolkien's enduring popularity. Some point to his exquisitely woven plots and subplots, some to his unforgettable characters. Some point to Tolkien's love of words and his genius for languages—the English language he wrote in and the languages of his own invention. Still others point to his utterly imaginative yet utterly vivid settings. While all these elements are unquestionably part of Tolkien's legacy, it might also be argued that the biggest reason his works have been so deeply loved, in both the previous century and the present one, is because they not only entertain readers—they also enrich their readers' lives and make them more meaningful.

For countless readers around the world, Tolkien's novels serve as those special kind of life-shaping stories that, in the words of Daniel Taylor, help tell us "who we are, why we are here, and what we are to do" (4). These special stories, as they are read and reread, can accompany us throughout the stages of life and help us see a pattern to our experience.

In this book, I follow the suggestion of Tolkien biographer Charles Moseley, who maintains that Tolkien's fictional world was animated by the author's Christian faith and Christian outlook. As Moseley has explained:

> Tolkien's Christian understanding of the nature of the world was fundamental to his thinking and to his major fiction. Neither propaganda nor allegory, at its root lies the Christian model of a world loved into being by a Creator, whose creatures have the free will to turn away from the harmony of that love to seek their own will and desires, rather than seeking to give themselves in love to others. This world is one of cause and consequence, where everything matters, however seemingly insignificant. (60)

J. R. R. Tolkien—without putting blinders on or sugarcoating the harsh realities of the human condition—offers readers a clear picture of the good, the true, and the beautiful. Through his fiction Tolkien points to something eternal, something that goes beyond the physical world and at the same time redeems and reenchants it.

We read Tolkien for many reasons, but perhaps above all, we read him because he helps us know that we live in a world still charged with meaning, even with magic. To those grown hungry for a world where people and their actions—no matter how seemingly small or insignificant—still have value, Tolkien's fictional works hold out, as author Michael White notes, "something irresistibly attractive" (2). Through his stories set in the imaginary world of Middle-earth, Tolkien helps us to see the sacramental nature of our own world, our own lives, and our own stories.

In this book I provide an exploration of the Christian vision that runs throughout Tolkien's first novel, *The Hobbit*. In chapter 1, I consider what it means to explore Christian themes in a book whose religious sensibilities are stated only indirectly. In the next three chapters, I examine three particular religious themes that were central to Tolkien's work— providence, purpose, and moral sensibility. In the fifth and final chapter, I consider the legacy that Tolkien has left us in *The Hobbit*.

And now I invite you to enter the sacred world of *The Hobbit* and to discover how Tolkien's faith impacted his fiction.

Devin Brown, Asbury University
Winter 2012

Chapter 1

AN "ESSENTIALLY" CHRISTIAN STORY

"In a Hole in the Ground There Lived a Hobbit"

In a letter he wrote to the poet W. H. Auden, John Ronald Reuel Tolkien describes the events that took place on a summer's day in 1930 as he was working at home in his study: "All I remember about the start of *The Hobbit* is sitting correcting School Certificate papers in the everlasting weariness of that annual task forced on impecunious academics with children. On a blank leaf I scrawled: 'In a hole in the ground there lived a hobbit.' I did not and do not know why. I did nothing about it, for a long time" (*Letters*, 215).

Had Professor Tolkien not needed the money that grading secondary school exams provided, had there not been so many of them, had there not been a blank page left in one exam booklet, there might never have been the story we know today as *The Hobbit*. Without the 1937 publication of *The Hobbit*, there certainly would never have been the public demand for a sequel, which resulted in the publication of *The Lord of the Rings* sixteen years later in 1953. Even with the now-famous opening line written, the whole thing might have ended there, except for the author's extraordinary interest in names and word origins. "Names always generate a story in my mind," he later explained (Carpenter, 175). "Eventually I thought I'd better find out what hobbits were like."

The Hobbit; or, There and Back Again tells the tale of Mr. Bilbo Baggins's unlikely meeting with thirteen dwarves and the even more unlikely adventure that follows as, under the occasional guidance of Gandalf the wizard, the company sets out on a perilous journey to reclaim a treasure from a dragon named Smaug. From the subtitle, readers know in advance that Bilbo will eventually make it back home. What they do not know is that the treasure our Mr. Baggins will return with will be quite different from the one he initially sets out to obtain.

In this brief description, *The Hobbit* does not sound like a very religious book. But in fact, Tolkien's Christian beliefs are a fundamental part of the story from start to finish and are certainly, in part, what was behind C. S. Lewis's observation that the story is "so true."

A Life of Deep Conviction

In 1953, looking back on his life at the age of sixty-one, Tolkien wrote to a friend about how deeply grateful he was for having been brought up in the Christian faith. "A faith," Tolkien concludes, "that has nourished me and taught me all the little that I know" (*Letters*, 172). As Joseph Pearce points out, for Tolkien this faith was not "an opinion to which one subscribed but a reality to which one submitted" (23).

On January 3, 1892, just three days into the new year, John Ronald Reuel was born in Bloemfontein in the Orange Free State, now South Africa, to Arthur and Mabel Tolkien. Two years later, the Tolkiens had a second baby son, whom they named Hilary. Economic opportunity as well as economic necessity had drawn Arthur and Mabel to relocate in the dust, heat, and treeless plains of Bloemfontein. The temperature proved to be particularly oppressive, especially for Ronald, as they called him. In 1895, Mabel sailed back to England with the two boys for an extended visit. While Arthur had plans to eventually join them, he became ill and died before these plans would materialize, leaving Mabel husbandless and the two young boys without a father.

Mabel Tolkien, now in part dependent upon help from relatives, rented a small, inexpensive cottage a mile past the southern borders of Birmingham in the village of Sarehole Mill, a location that, much later, would provide Tolkien with his pastoral setting of the Shire as well as his lifelong opposition to the industrialization and mechanization that were gradually overtaking the countryside. As Tolkien biographer Humphrey Carpenter notes, Christianity began to play "an increasingly important part" in Mabel Tolkien's life following her husband's death (31). Though the family had been Anglican, in 1900 she and her two sons converted to Catholicism.

On November 14, 1904, Ronald Tolkien received the second major blow of his young life: his mother died of complications related to diabetes. She was thirty-four. He was twelve.

What effect did the loss of his beloved mother—who had also been his schoolteacher, spiritual director, and close companion—have on Tolkien's later development as a writer of a certain kind of fantasy literature? Any speculation would be purely conjecture and precisely the sort of psychoanalyzing about authors that Tolkien hated. Still, a set of extraordinary coincidences confronts us that can at the least be labeled remarkable. Mabel Tolkien died in November 1904 when Ronald was twelve. Flora Lewis died in August 1908 when Clive Staples Lewis was just short of his tenth birthday. Helen MacDonald died in 1832 when her son George was eight years old. Three of the greatest fantasy writers in the English language all suffered the childhood loss of their mothers, a painful loss that sent them to imaginative realms for consolation.

About the influence his mother had on his lifelong vocation in philology, Tolkien would write, "My interest in languages was derived solely from my mother. . . . She knew German, and gave me my first lessons in it. She was also interested in etymology, and aroused my interest in this; and also in alphabets and handwriting" (*Letters*, 377). Even more important than her role in encouraging her older son's interest in linguistics, Mabel was instrumental in starting him on a path of deep, abiding faith. Regarding the profound and genuine belief that he had embraced since childhood, Tolkien later wrote, "That I owe to my mother" (*Letters*, 172).

With both parents gone, guardianship of the boys was given to Father Francis Morgan, their priest at the Birmingham Oratory, who took charge of making sure that Ronald and Hilary received a proper education. In the coming years, Tolkien would graduate from Oxford and fight in World War I. He would marry and have children of his own. He would become a university professor, first at Leeds and then at Oxford. All during this time, he continued with pious devotion to pray, attend church, and receive Communion. He raised his growing family to share his deep convictions.

About a third of the way into his roughly three-hundred-page biography, Humphrey Carpenter recounts how Tolkien moved back to Oxford in 1925 to accept the professorship he would hold until his retirement in 1959. Then Carpenter writes, "And after this, you might say, nothing else really happened" (118). Carpenter continues, "It was the ordinary unremarkable life led by countless other scholars. . . . And that would be that—apart from the strange fact that during these years when 'nothing happened' he wrote two books which have become world best-sellers, books that have captured the imagination and influenced the thinking of several million readers" (118).

In the curious creation of these two books—*The Hobbit* and *The Lord of the Rings*, which now have had more than a hundred million readers each—we could say, using words from *Hamlet*, "even in that was heaven ordinant." In a real-life story as fascinating as the imaginary ones they would later write, J. R. R. Tolkien and C. S. Lewis became friends, Tolkien became instrumental in Lewis's conversion to Christianity, and then Lewis became instrumental in Tolkien's writing his great works. Together they formed the Inklings, the close-knit Oxford reading and writing group that met in Lewis's rooms and at a pub named The Eagle and Child. It was at these meetings that the early versions of *The Hobbit* and *The Lord of the Rings* were first read aloud, critiqued, and made into what they are today.

In a letter written in 1965, two years after Lewis's death, Tolkien would describe the "unpayable debt" he owed Lewis, explaining: "He was for long my only audience. Only from him did I ever get the idea that my 'stuff' could be more than a private hobby. But for his interest and unceasing eagerness for more I should never have brought *The Lord of the Rings* to a conclusion" (*Letters*, 362).

In chapter 3 of *The Hobbit*, the company arrives at Rivendell for a much-needed rest. The narrator breaks in to comment that "things that are good to have and days that are good to spend are soon told about, and not much to listen to" (48). Unlike Lewis, Tolkien did not go through a dark and stormy phase of atheism followed by a return to belief. Nor did Tolkien became a great spokesperson for the faith, as Lewis did, although Tolkien did serve as one of the translators for the Jerusalem Bible. Tolkien's faith journey  can be said to more resemble "days that are good to spend" than a journey to the Lonely Mountain and so is soon told about.

While there is no way to paint an adequate portrait of his life of quiet devotion, perhaps two further glimpses will serve to suggest the vitality of Tolkien's belief. In a letter written to a longtime friend and correspondent in 1969, Tolkien offers these words of belief in a God who hears and answers prayer, who comforts, and who calls his followers to be a comfort:

"I am perturbed by and sorry for your afflictions. . . . I pray for you—because I have a feeling (more near a certainty) that God, for some ineffable reason which to us may seem almost like humor, is so curiously ready to answer the prayers of the *least* worthy of his suppliants—if they pray for others" (*Letters*, 401). The Tolkiens knew firsthand the promise found in James 5:16 that "the effectual fervent prayer of a righteous man availeth much," as they were firmly convinced that one of their children had been cured of a heart ailment through prayer.

In another letter, this one written to Camilla Unwin, his publisher's young daughter, Tolkien was asked to describe the purpose of life as part of Camilla's school project. The chief purpose of life for all of us, Tolkien responded, is to "increase according to our capacity our knowledge of God by all the means we have, and to be moved by it to praise and thanks" (*Letters*, 400).

The author of *The Hobbit* and *The Lord of the Rings* saw the ultimate goal of life—his life and everyone's life—to be an ever-increasing knowledge of God, the kind of knowledge that leads to praise and thanks. Tolkien's readers might add one more response to his list, one that Tolkien's fiction helps to kindle and keep alive in their own lives: hope—the kind of hope that, as Legolas tells Gimli in *The Return of the King*, is born when all is forlorn.

Essentially Christian Works

On December 2, 1953, with apologies for its unfriendly, formal appearance, Tolkien typed out a fairly short, five-paragraph letter to his good friend Father Robert Murray. Though he had enjoyed drawing and calligraphy throughout his life, now at age sixty-one, Tollers, as he was known to his friends, was finding that holding a pen for any length of time was tiring and painful. So more and more, even for personal letters, he used the small manual typewriter kept in the cluttered study of the house on Sandfield Road where he and his wife, Edith, lived just outside of Oxford.

In the years that followed, this letter would become well-known among Tolkien enthusiasts.

Robert Murray had come to Oxford nine years earlier, in 1944, and shortly afterward, to a large measure through Tolkien's influence, had converted and was received into the church. Going on to become a Jesuit, he had remained a close friend of both the Tolkiens and had helped the author by reading and commenting on parts of the galley proofs and the typescript for *The Lord of the Rings*. After a long and difficult genesis, the massive work was finally about to be published, with *The Fellowship of the Ring* and *The Two Towers* to come out a year later in 1954 and *The Return of the King* to follow in 1955. Tolkien's letter was a reply to several comments Father Murray had provided, among them Murray's claim that the work had left him with strong sense of a "positive compatibility with the order of Grace" (*Letters*, 171–72).

Tolkien wrote back that he thought he understood exactly what Murray meant, and then, after a few brief intervening remarks, made his now-famous, often-quoted, and much-discussed declaration: "*The Lord of the Rings* is of course a fundamentally religious and Catholic work; unconsciously so at first, but consciously in the revision" (*Letters*, 172).

The Lord of the Rings is a fundamentally religious work—and not just in a vague, subconscious way, but intentionally and *consciously* so, as its author revised the story again and again in the years leading up to its publication.

At first glance this may seem a strange statement, one that despite having the author's own word on it, may be difficult for many who have read the work to accept. As Fleming Rutledge has rightly pointed out, on the surface Middle-earth is "a curiously nonreligious world" (6). A careful look reveals practically none of the elements we typically associate with religion. The word *God* is never mentioned directly in either *The Hobbit* or *The Lord of the Rings*. Both stories are set in a time that is pre-Christian and even pre–Old Testament. Thus readers find no cathedrals, temples, or churches; no priests, ministers, or clergy; no Bibles; and no liturgy. Save for those who gave devotion to Sauron in the Dark Years; and Gollum, who bows and offers homage to Shelob, there is no mention of worship. Except for two vague incidents, there are no prayers. In appendix A at the end of *The Return of the King*, readers find a reference to the "One" who placed the Valar in guardianship over Middle-earth (1013), and, in Arwen's farewell words to Aragorn, a reference to the "One" who gave the gift of death to men (1038).

So what could its creator possibly have meant when he said *The Lord of the Rings* is a fundamentally religious work?

The key to understanding Tolkien's statement to Father Murray hinges on the word *fundamentally*. Paraphrasing Tolkien, we could say that *The Lord of the Rings* is in its fundamentals or at its foundations a religious work. In "The Quest Hero," his seminal essay on *The Lord of the Rings*, the great poet W. H. Auden expresses this idea in slightly different words, stating that "the unstated presuppositions of the whole work are Christian" (44).

Tolkien's use of the phrase "fundamentally religious" is made more precise as he goes on to explain to Father Murray: "That is why I have not put in, or have cut out, practically all references to anything like 'religion,' to cults or practices, in the imaginary world" (*Letters*, 172). Tolkien makes clear his strategy, writing that "the religious element is absorbed into the story."

In an interview, Tolkien told the American scholar Clyde Kilby, "I am a Christian and of course what I write will be from that essential viewpoint" ("Mythic," 141). Here, instead of the word *fundamentally*, Tolkien uses the word *essential*. Tolkien's writings—*The Hobbit* and *The Lord of the Rings*—are in their essence, at their core, Christian works, but only at their core, not on the surface. The Christian viewpoint, and Tolkien's own words, tells us that he has included one, has been absorbed, has been embedded into his stories and so, except for a few very minor instances, cannot be seen on the surface.

Nearly five years after his famous letter to Father Murray, Tolkien expanded on this idea in a letter dated October 25, 1958, in which he responded to a number of questions Deborah Webster had sent him. There the author tells her, "I am a Christian" and then adds in parentheses "which can be deduced from my stories" (*Letters*, 288). Here the word *deduced* is key, making it clear that the Christian element in Tolkien's stories is present but is not directly evident and must be deduced. In addition, the author tells us it can be deduced from the stories themselves, not something else. While Tolkien's letters, lectures, and other external materials can shed additional light on the Christian aspect in his fiction, if we look below the surface, we can find it in and deduce it from the actual stories. As one of Tolkien's fans put it in a letter to the author, "You . . . create a world in which some sort of faith seems to be everywhere without a visible source, like light from an invisible lamp" (*Letters*, 413). We could say that Tolkien's fiction is permeated with his beliefs, that the Christian element has been infused into the story.

While some readers discern the Christian aspects in Tolkien's stories, many others do not. Does someone need to be Christian to enjoy Tolkien's works? Certainly not. As Joseph Pearce has noted, readers can enjoy Tolkien's fiction "without sharing the beliefs which gave it birth," as is "evident from the many millions who have read and enjoyed Tolkien's books without sharing his Christianity" (100). In fact, one of the most remarkable aspects about *The Hobbit* and *The Lord of the Rings* is their universal appeal—their unique ability to charm and inspire people all over the world, young and old, from many differing backgrounds. At the same time, Pearce claims that to fully understand Tolkien's fiction, serious readers "cannot afford to ignore Tolkien's philosophical and theological beliefs, central as they are to his whole conception of Middle-earth and the struggles within it" (100).

While it is clear that the goal of some writers of fantasy is simply to amuse and delight their readers, this was not Tolkien's primary goal. The main purpose of Tolkien's stories of imaginary beings in an imaginary world was to provide a better understanding of our world and the real beings who inhabit it. In an article titled "The Hero Is a Hobbit," which appeared in the *New York Times*, W. H. Auden claims that Tolkien "holds up the mirror to the only nature we know, our own."

In an essay about Tolkien's fiction titled "The Dethronement of Power," C. S. Lewis posed the question:

"Why, if you have a serious comment to make on the real life of men, must you do it by talking about a phantasmagoric never-never land of your own?" (14). Lewis's answer was that placing the elements of this world into a mythic world, as Tolkien did, allows us to "see them more clearly" (15), in ways that are more poignant and more powerful. When we journey to Middle-earth, Lewis concludes, "we do not retreat from reality: we rediscover it" (15).

Tolkien himself described *The Hobbit* as "a study of simple ordinary man, neither artistic nor noble and heroic" (*Letters*, 159). While his stories are among the most entertaining works of fiction ever written, Tolkien's intent was that they would also serve a more serious purpose.

"I Cordially Dislike Allegory in All Its Manifestations"

If Tolkien's 1953 letter to Father Murray contains the most frequently quoted statement the author made about his writing—that *The Lord of the Rings* is a fundamentally religious work—his next most commonly cited statement about his stories can be found in the "Foreword to the Second Edition" of *The Fellowship of the Ring*. Among his responses to the many comments and inquiries he had received, Tolkien especially felt the need to reply to those readers who were convinced that the War of the Ring was an allegory for World War II, that Sauron represented Hitler, and that the ring must be the atomic bomb.

In the foreword, the author states that readers were mistaken if they thought specific elements in his stories were intended to represent specific elements in the real world in this kind of one-to-one equivalence. To all those hunting for this special sort of allegorical, inner meaning in his work, Tolkien makes it clear there is none. "I cordially dislike allegory," Tolkien declares in the foreword, "in all its manifestations" (xv).

Tolkien's works are fundamentally Christian. They are not Christian allegories.

While people use *allegory* to mean a number of different things, some of them quite vague, the term actually has a rather precise meaning. In a letter written to his publisher on July 31, 1947, Tolkien notes that some people may confuse an allegory with a story that simply has a moral. Tolkien writes: "Do not let Rayner suspect 'Allegory.' There is 'moral,' I suppose, in any tale worth telling. But that is not the same thing" (*Letters*, 121). An allegory is a story that makes use of a cluster of symbols, objects, or events that have a literal presence in the story but are also intended to directly represent something else outside the story and thus to point to a secondary meaning. While all the time there is a literal or surface meaning within the story, the author of an allegory is using those surface elements only to point to the "real" meaning outside the story.

The parable of the sower found in the Gospels is a good illustration of how allegory works. Jesus tells of a man who goes out to sow seed. Some seed falls on the path, some on rocky ground, some among thorns, and some upon good soil. As Jesus explained, the seed symbolizes something beyond the story—the word of God—and each of the various places the seed falls also has a secondary meaning. As Tolkien scholar Tom Shippey has noted, the "basic operation" of allegory is "to start making equations" (*Road*, 43). In this vein, we could say that the seed that falls on the path equals one kind of people who hear the word, the seed that falls on the rocky soil equals another kind, and so on.

Another famous allegory is Pharaoh's dream from the Old Testament. Pharaoh tells Joseph that in his dream he is standing by the side of the river. Suddenly seven fat cows come up from the water and graze in the meadow. Then seven thin cows come out of the river and eat the seven fat cows. Joseph explains that the seven fat cows represent seven years of plenty for Egypt and the seven thin cows represent seven years of famine that will follow, wiping out the seven years of abundance.

Perhaps the most famous allegory in English literature is Bunyan's *Pilgrim's Progress*, in which Christian's journey to the Celestial City equals or represents the soul's struggle toward heaven, and all the other main elements Bunyan includes have similar correspondences.

In allegories, the surface or literal story is not particularly compelling, nor does it need to be since it is not the author's focus. The story in an allegory is simply a means of illustrating something else. In both the parable of the sower and Pharaoh's dream, we see that the only reason for the literal story is to point to its secondary meaning. To claim that Tolkien's stories are allegories is to imply that they are not worthy to be read, enjoyed, and studied on their own. To mistakenly see Tolkien's stories as allegories is to take a secret-decoder-ring approach in the hope of revealing their "hidden" meaning.

In a letter dated November 17, 1957, Tolkien again makes it clear that he was not writing the kind of work where one thing equals another. He states: "There is *no* 'symbolism' or conscious allegory in my story. Allegory of the sort 'five wizards = five senses' is wholly foreign to my way of thinking. . . . To ask if the Orcs 'are' Communists is to me as sensible as asking if Communists are Orcs" (*Letters*, 262).

But, it might be argued, isn't Sauron—called the Necromancer in *The Hobbit*—in some ways like Hitler? Don't they share a number of similarities? Of course they do. Sauron will share similarities with many tyrants from our world. While there are some ways that Sauron and Hitler will be alike, this is very different from saying that Sauron represents or equals Hitler. As Tolkien explains in the foreword to the second edition, "I think that many confuse 'applicability' with 'allegory'" (xv).

While someone might say, "I see a lot of Hitler in Sauron," or "The ring shares some aspects with the atomic bomb," these connections are being made by the reader, not by the author, and are the very thing Tolkien means by applicability. To say that we can find similarities is very different from saying that the author intended a one-to-one allegory. To find elements in the story that are applicable to the real world means the author has done a good job portraying the human situation.

In his preface to *The Screwtape Letters*, C. S. Lewis points out, "There are two equal and opposite errors into which our race can fall about the devils. One is to disbelieve in their existence. The other is to believe, and to feel an excessive and unhealthy interest in them" (ix). In a similar vein, it could be said that there are two equal and opposite errors into which readers can fall when exploring the relationship between Tolkien's faith and his fiction. One is to totally ignore the Christian aspects in Tolkien's stories. The other is to find Christian aspects everywhere, in places the author has not put them. As Professor Clyde Kilby has rightly noted, "No real lover of Tolkien's fiction would want it turned into sermons, no matter how cleverly preached" (*Tolkien*, 79).

In his review titled "Tolkien's *The Lord of the Rings*," C. S. Lewis acknowledges that some readers may want to "identify the Ring with the hydrogen bomb, and Mordor with Russia" (89). But using Treebeard's favorite word,

Lewis labels any attempt to set up these kind of equivalencies—where this equals this and that equals that—as "hasty." In a chapter titled "Second Meanings" from *Reflections on the Psalms*, Lewis makes a similar point about readers' tendency to find all sorts of far-fetched, allegorical meanings the authors never intended—especially in works of fantasy:

> As we know, almost anything can be read into any book if you are determined enough. This will be especially impressed on anyone who has written fantastic fiction. He will find reviewers, both favorable and hostile, reading into his stories all manner of allegorical meanings which he never intended. (Some of the allegories thus imposed on my own books have been so ingenious and interesting that I often wish I had thought of them myself.) Apparently it is impossible for the wit of man to devise a narrative in which the wit of some other man cannot, and with some plausibility, find a hidden sense. (99–100)

In this book, I will make the case that *The Hobbit* is a fundamentally Christian work where we can see Tolkien's faith reflected in his fiction. I will not be arguing that the Necromancer (or Smaug) represents Satan, that the ring is a symbol of original sin, that Gandalf equals Christ, or that any of the various traitors are Judas Iscariot. While there may be similarities that evoke associations in the reader's mind, the proper claim to make in these cases is something like *parallels, echoes, resembles, mirrors,* or *reflects*, not *represents, symbolizes, corresponds to, equals,* or *is*.

Colin Duriez has written that Tolkien has an importance as a Christian writer because his fiction "embodies Christian meaning," and does this by "recovering and restoring a Christian way of seeing reality," even for readers who do not share his beliefs (229). By looking for the Christian principles that can be found at the center of *The Hobbit*, we also discover one of the reasons this book has been and continues to be so widely popular seventy-five years after its original publication in 1937—and so cherished.

The Religious Element Is Absorbed into the Story: Some Thoughts on Why

Eleven months after the letter where he described the fundamentally religious nature of his work, Tolkien wrote to Father Murray again to respond to further observations. "I have purposely kept all allusions to the highest matters down to mere hints," Tolkien explains (*Letters*, 201). These mere hints will be perceptible to only the "most attentive" readers. God and his angels will only "peep through."

Why include all allusions to the highest matters as mere hints? Why have the religious element only peep through the story and not be included more directly?

First, it was against Tolkien's nature to be too explicit, to write too directly, about the things he felt deepest about—

and this would especially include matters of faith. In fact, this was one of the aspects he disliked most about C. S. Lewis's writing. As Tom Shippey observes, the "overtly Christian message" of Lewis's Narnia books was a major point of contention between the two authors (359). Tolkien thought Lewis, a layman, went too far in writing about issues of faith, issues that should be reserved for the clergy. Alan Jacobs describes the difference this way: "What Lewis took upon himself was, in Tolkien's judgment, none of Lewis's business" (199).

While Tolkien had a problem with Lewis's more overtly Christian works, Lewis had no problem with Tolkien's practice of making the Christian elements more implicit. In a letter dated August 14, 1954, Lewis seems to have had this contrast between himself and Tolkien in mind, as he tells a correspondent:

> I think you have a mistaken idea of a Christian writer's duty. We must use the talent we have, not the talents we haven't. We must not of course write anything that will flatter lust, pride, or ambition. But we needn't all write patently moral or theological work. Indeed, work whose Christianity is latent may do quite as much good and may reach some whom the more obvious religious work would scare away. (*Collected Letters*, 502)

Numerous readers would attest to the fact that this latent Christianity in Tolkien's fiction is able to reach them and do them "much good" in a manner that more obvious religious works did not.

In a letter written in July 1972, Tolkien touched on the death of his wife and on his reticence to fully give voice to the profound loss he felt. In this letter, Tolkien offers another possible clue about why he chose to write about his religious beliefs in a less-than-explicit way. It was simply his nature, Tolkien explained, to express his deepest feelings only in "tales and myths" (*Letters*, 420).

Even if it had been his nature to be more direct, Tolkien firmly believed there was a vital role for the implicit or unstated in a story. In a letter written to his publisher complaining about the blurb for the paperback edition of *The Hobbit*, Tolkien summarizes what *The Hobbit* and *The Lord of the Rings* are about. He makes it clear that his two great works were not intended to be merely stories of growth through experience, but tales involving graced and ordained individuals who were guided by an emissary of someone he leaves unnamed. But then the author further comments that "saying such things" and making them explicit risks spoiling these very aspects (*Letters*, 365).

Biographer Humphrey Carpenter offers this explanation for a God who is both present and unseen in Middle-earth:

> Some have puzzled over the relation between Tolkien's stories and his Christianity, and have found it difficult to understand how a devout Roman Catholic could write with such conviction about a world where God is not wor-

shipped. . . . Tolkien cast his mythology in this form because he wanted it to be remote and strange, and yet at the same time *not to be a lie.* He wanted the mythological and legendary stories to express his own moral view of the universe. . . . So while God is present in Tolkien's universe, He remains unseen. (99)

What Makes a Fictional Work Christian?

David Mills has observed, "It is hard to explain what makes a story a Christian story. . . . One has to derive a work's Christianity from the assumptions it makes and the sort of world it describes" (22). Some stories with narrowly defined Christian characters and overly moralistic Christian messages may sometimes feel more *Christianized* than authentically Christian. One way to approach the question of what makes a work of fiction Christian may be to briefly look at a very different kind of fiction.

The year was 1957. With the release of *The Return of the King* two years earlier in 1955, the groundswell of public opinion about *The Lord of the Rings* was very slowly beginning to build, one passionate reader at a time. Meanwhile, in France, another more celebrated author had just published a short story titled "The Guest." In its own circle of admirers, "The Guest" would become as famous as any work of

Tolkien. Along with a series of works that included *The Stranger*, it would help earn their author, Albert Camus, the Nobel Prize in Literature.

"The Guest" centers around a difficult decision thrust upon a French schoolmaster named Daru who is stationed in Algeria. While the word *existentialist* is never explicitly used in "The Guest," all of the existentialist assumptions are present. Daru's dilemma is whether or not to deliver an Arab who has committed murder to the French authorities. With no objective right or wrong, he has no guidelines on which to base his decision. He will not be rewarded or recognized for making the correct choice—there is no correct choice and no God to reward it. Any decision he makes will have no moral significance beyond his own set of values and will be made entirely on his own. In the end, Daru simply releases the Arab, instructing him to find shelter among his own people. Daru's action proves futile. Rather than accepting his freedom, the man takes the road to prison. The story ends with this stark existentialist statement of man's isolation in an empty, meaningless universe: "Daru looked at the sky, the plateau, and, beyond, the invisible lands stretching all the way to the sea. In this vast landscape he had loved so much, he was alone" (109).

Just as we call "The Guest" existentialist because it presents a fundamentally existential worldview, we can also classify Tolkien's fiction as Christian because it presents a fundamentally Christian worldview. If Daru's education is to learn that he is ultimately alone and insignificant, Bilbo and Frodo learn the exact opposite. While Daru finds himself isolated and alienated in a world that is spiritually vacant, the characters in Tolkien's fiction find that they live in a world charged with a divine presence and that they are connected in ways they never imagined—to one another, to the rest of Middle-earth, and to something beyond Middle-earth.

With the observations from this chapter as a backdrop, we can now move on to explore the Providence, purpose, and moral landscape in the Christian world of *The Hobbit*.

Chapter 2

"LUCK OF AN UNUSUAL KIND": PROVIDENCE IN *THE HOBBIT*

In chapter 3 of *The Hobbit*, Gandalf, Bilbo, and the dwarves finally reach Rivendell, where they enjoy a much-needed rest after the first leg of the journey and their near catastrophe with the trolls. Their clothes are mended along with their bruises, tempers, and hopes, and their plans are improved with the best advice.

Elrond, who knows about runes of every kind, inspects Glamdring and Orcrist, the swords Gandalf and Thorin took from the trolls' plunder. He then asks to see their map.

Holding it up in the light of that night's crescent moon, Elrond finds—to everyone's surprise—that additional letters have now suddenly become visible. These moon-letters, we are told, can be seen only by the light of a moon, which appears in the exact same season and has the exact same shape as the day on which the letters were originally written.

Elrond just happens to be looking at the map at the one exact moment when the otherwise invisible moon-letters can be seen. To highlight the event's extremely coincidental nature, Tolkien's narrator tells us there would not be another such astronomical alignment until "goodness knows when" (50).

Does Tolkien want readers to believe that this unlikely coincidence has really come about by chance? Or is he suggesting by this highly improbable incident, and others like it, that there is another force at work in Middle-earth besides sheer luck? This is a question that Tolkien has us return to again and again in *The Hobbit*. And by the end of the story, it is clear what the author's position is.

The word *luck* appears twenty-five times in *The Hobbit*, *luckily* is used eleven times, and the word *lucky* nine times. We find these luck-related words used by Tolkien so regularly that readers may begin to wonder if the author is suggesting by this frequency that there is more than mere luck at work, that what may seem like luck at the time is really the hand of Providence.

In chapter 1, Gandalf tells the dwarves that if they think he made a mistake in choosing Bilbo, they can stop at thirteen and have all the "bad luck" they like (19), thus framing the whole quest under the question of luck. In chapter 5 we are told Bilbo is saved by "pure luck" when he needs more time to figure out Gollum's riddle but can only stammer "Time! Time!" which is actually the answer (72). In chapter 8, Tolkien has Gandalf tell Bilbo and the dwarves they have gotten beyond the mountains "by good management *and* good luck" (104), and the author's use of italics here emphasizes the critical role this seeming good luck has played.

In his farewell before the borders of Mirkwood, Gandalf tells the company that with a "tremendous slice of luck" they may reach the other side (126), something they apparently have, since they finally make it to Lake-town. While they are in the forest, Bilbo becomes separated from the group, and Tolkien reports that Dori stumbles upon him by "sheer luck" (139). Two chapters later, readers are told "luck of an unusual kind" is with Bilbo (161), in this case because although wood-elves are unaffected by most wines, the variety that the chief guard has consumed happens to be a very rare vintage that induces a deep and undisturbable slumber. A few pages after he and the dwarves escape through the water gate, Bilbo shivers in the water with the barrels, wondering if he will die of the cold, but then we are told the "luck turned" as a hidden root steadies his barrel, so he can scramble on top (167).

In addition to the frequency with which Tolkien uses some variation of the word *luck*, *The Hobbit*'s plot turns on a series of coincidental events that seem particularly lucky, even if the word *luck* is not mentioned. During the riddling game with Gollum, it seems extraordinarily fortunate that a fish happens to jump out of the water and onto Bilbo's toes, because *fish* is the solution to the riddle that Gollum has just asked.

The moon-letters Elrond discovers on the map state that the keyhole to the door on the mountain will be visible only when the thrush knocks on the last light of Durin's Day. Thorin explains that Durin's Day occurs when the last moon of autumn and the sun are visible in the sky together, but adds that the dwarves are now unable to guess when such a moment will reoccur. So again it is apparently just by luck that in chapter 11 Bilbo just happens to be sitting by the doorstep at just the right moment to witness the brief appearance of the keyhole, allowing them to get inside. "Dwarf-doors are not made to be seen when shut," Gimli explains when the company reaches the doors to Moria in *The Fellowship of the Ring* (296). If the secret way to reveal them is forgotten, Gimli states, even their own masters will not be able to find them. If Bilbo had not been there at that precise moment to see the keyhole appear, the secret door to the Lonely Mountain would have remained shut forever.

In addition, it seems very lucky for Bilbo and the dwarves that there is even sunlight in those crucial seconds. After appearing briefly to bring out the door's faint tracing, the sun then dips behind a cloud belt. But then, at the very last moment, one ray of sun escapes "like a finger" through a slit in the clouds, causing the keyhole to come into view (190).

In framing his request that the hobbit go down to Smaug's lair and spy on the dragon in chapter 12, Thorin makes note of the fact that Bilbo is possessed of good luck "far exceeding the usual allowance" (191). Bilbo responds that somehow he thinks he will not refuse. "Perhaps I have begun to trust my luck more than I used to in the old days," the hobbit states. In *The Return of the King*, Tolkien has Sam use similar words as he is deciding whether to risk taking the road again as they cross Mordor. Sam tells Frodo, "Trust to luck again! It nearly failed us last time, but it didn't quite" (914). In both cases, the gravity of the circumstances suggests that Tolkien is pointing to a trust in something beyond mere random accident.

In chapter 12 of *The Hobbit*, it seems an odd chance that the old thrush just happens to be nearby listening when Bilbo reveals that Smaug has a bare place where he is vulnerable, and just happens to be one of the last of those who can understand human speech. It certainly proves very lucky that the bird is there at just that moment, if *lucky* is the proper word. Because the thrush overhears Bilbo's news, the bird is able to tell Bard where to shoot his final arrow and so bring down the dragon and save the people of Lake-town. Tolkien has Thorin underscore the chance coincidence that this thrush could be one of those who understand human speech. The dwarf tells Bilbo that the bird is *maybe* the last of an ancient breed tamed by his father and *might even be* one of those who were alive then, several hundred years ago, who took messages to the Men of the Lake and could speak their language.

Balin concludes that it may be "a mercy and a blessing" to know about Smaug's bare patch (205), and his words stand out for two reasons. First, they are not the kind of words one of the dwarves would typically use, and so readers' attention is drawn to them. Second, here, in place of the word *lucky*, Tolkien uses words with strong spiritual connotations. In *The Return of the King*, Tolkien has Frodo use a similar phrase that points beyond luck to something more. As they ponder whether it is safe to drink the water they find in Mordor, Frodo says to Sam, "I think we'll trust our luck together, Sam, or our blessing" (900).

From the start, Bilbo has been associated with luck so often that readers may begin to hear hints of something greater, of some benevolent agency at work behind the scenes. Bilbo is chosen as the lucky number. In riddling with Smaug, Bilbo calls himself Luckwearer, and Smaug calls the hobbit Mr. Lucky Number. In the book's final chapter, when Bilbo is discovered to have survived the Battle of Five Armies, Gandalf expresses delight at seeing the hobbit alive and adds, "I began to wonder if even your luck would see you through!" (258).

But does Tolkien really want readers to believe that, all throughout the story, it has been just luck at work seeing Bilbo through every difficulty?

Biased Fortune or Something Else?

None of the occurrences of luck in *The Hobbit* can match the apparent coincidence of Bilbo's finding and picking up the ring that Gollum has lost. After becoming separated from the others during their escape from the goblins, Bilbo crawls blindly along in the tunnels beneath the Misty Mountains. Readers are told that suddenly the hobbit's hand touches what feels like a tiny ring of cold metal. Given the huge, cavernous spaces of the goblin kingdom, the miles of mazelike passageways, the tiny fraction of the tunnels that Bilbo traverses, the fact that he can see nothing, and the extremely small space where his hand touches down, to many readers Bilbo's coincidental finding of the ring may seem like too much of a coincidence, like simply too much luck. As if recognizing this fact, Tolkien's narrator states, "A magic ring . . . ! He had heard of such things, . . . but it was hard to believe that he had found one, by accident" (79).

It was hard to believe that he had found one, by accident. Scholar Colin Manlove agrees and argues that there are too many implausible coincidences like this one in Tolkien's writing. Manlove maintains that Tolkien's overdependence on luck is a weakness on the author's part.

"There is a glaring feature of Tolkien's fantasy which critics have tended to play down or ignore," Manlove writes in the section on Tolkien in his book *Modern Fantasy: Five Studies* (180). This glaring feature of Tolkien's fantasy—and by "glaring feature" Manlove means "glaring flaw"—is "the continued presence of a biased fortune." Although he writes about this problem primarily as it can be found in *The Lord of the Rings*, Manlove's criticism extends to *The Hobbit* as well. In Tolkien's writing, Manlove finds "a whole skein of apparent coincidences and luck," with many one-in-a-million chances and frequent near miraculous events (182). Manlove insists, "It is not moral will but luck which is the architect of success" (183). He argues that Tolkien's use of luck as a method to solve problems so degrades the conflict with evil that it becomes "mere posturing in a rigged boat" (183).

But there is another way to interpret all the seeming coincidence in *The Hobbit*. A careful reading of the text suggests that we are not supposed to see simply random chance at work. As David Mills has suggested, Tolkien gives his readers not "a horribly contrived plot," but "a study in Providence" (23). Bilbo is not merely lucky—he is being guided by a force larger than himself, a force that cares about his well-being and cares that his mission succeeds.

On *The Hobbit*'s final page, a place of particular promi-
nence, the author speaks through Gandalf to explicitly make
the point hinted at all along. The wizard asks Bilbo, "You
don't really suppose, do you, that all your adventure and
escapes were managed by mere luck, just for your sole benefit?" (272). Bilbo agrees with Gandalf's final statement, with
a grateful "Thank goodness!" Readers are meant to learn
what Bilbo learns and to conclude along with Bilbo that his
adventures and escapes were managed by something that
may have seemed like mere luck at the time but is something
far greater.

A look at an earlier version of the story—published in
The History of The Hobbit—makes Tolkien's intentions here
even clearer. In the 1933 manuscript that Tolkien loaned to
Lewis, he has Gandalf say: "After all you don't really suppose, do you, that all your adventures and all your *wonderful*
escapes were managed by *you yourself*, do you?" (Rateliff
692–93, changes italicized).

If, as Tolkien tells us through Gandalf, all Bilbo's adventures and escapes were not managed by mere luck nor by just
Bilbo himself, then by what or whom? In a letter Tolkien
offers this additional statement about the veiled power at
work in both *The Hobbit* and *The Lord of the Rings*:

> The story and its sequel are . . . about the achievements of
> specially graced and gifted individuals. I would say . . . "by
> ordained individuals, inspired and guided by an Emissary
> to ends beyond their individual education and enlargement."

This is clear in *The Lord of the Rings*; but it is present, if veiled, in *The Hobbit* from the beginning, and is alluded to in Gandalf's last words. (*Letters*, 365)

In these words Tolkien raises but chooses not to explicitly answer the question of who it is that has *graced*, *gifted*, and *ordained* his heroes. Nor does the author reveal who it is that Gandalf is an *emissary* for. But he does make it clear that this element of special grace has been present in *The Hobbit* from its very beginning and is what Gandalf's final words point to.

Gandalf's last words—"You don't really suppose, do you, that all your adventure and escapes were managed by mere luck, just for your sole benefit?"—are the last comment Tolkien makes in *The Hobbit* about the issue of Bilbo's so-called luck. But in the second chapter of *The Fellowship of the Ring* we are given more information about the ring, which has now passed on to Frodo. There Gandalf recounts its long background and finally comes to what he calls "the strangest event in the whole history of the Ring so far: Bilbo's arrival just at that time, and putting his hand on it, blindly, in the dark" (54).

In the words Tolkien gives Gandalf here—"just at that time" and "blindly, in the dark"—we again hear the implication that this strange event is simply too strange to have happened just by luck. Then Gandalf makes explicit what has been implied. He tells Frodo that the ring was picked up by the "most unlikely" person imaginable, Bilbo from the

Shire, not by blind luck or random chance, but because there was "more than one power at work" (54). Gandalf extends this point, but only a bit, stating that behind Bilbo's finding the ring there was "something else at work, beyond any design of the Ring-maker." We are not told what or who this something else is, but the use of the phrase "beyond any design of the Ring-maker" suggests the existence of a design crafted by someone else.

A similar point is made by Tom Bombadil in *The Fellowship of the Ring* several chapters later. When Merry and Pippin get caught by Old Man Willow and are about to be squeezed in two, Tom seemingly just happens to be in the area and arrives in the nick of time to save them. At supper that night, when Frodo asks if it was just chance that brought him, Tom replies, "Just chance brought me then, if chance you call it. It was no plan of mine" (123). In the response "if chance you call it," we hear the implication that Tom does not call it chance. His statement "It was no plan of mine" suggests that his providential arrival was, in fact, a plan of someone else who goes unnamed. At the Council of Elrond, Gandalf uses words similar to Tom's to describe the coincidental driving of Sauron from Mirkwood the very year that Bilbo came across the ring. "A strange chance," Gandalf calls it, "if chance it was" (244). In *The Two Towers*, after Pippin's nearly disastrous look into the Palantir, Tolkien has Gandalf again make plain that what may appear as luck or chance is in fact something greater. The wizard tells Pippin,

"You have been saved, and all your friends too, mainly by good fortune, as it is called" (579).

Clearly, Gandalf does not call it good fortune. He has a very different name for it.

An Encouraging Thought

So it was not mere luck that led Bilbo to the ring or that managed all his harrowing adventures and narrow escapes. There was an unseen hand with specific intentions, for Bilbo and for Middle-earth, helping all along. What, if anything, can we say about this unseen hand? It certainly does not solve all of Bilbo's problems for him. It does not ensure that his life is always pleasant and comfortable. This outside force always seems to help Bilbo when he needs help but not always when he wants it. It seldom, if ever, works in ways he could have predicted.

In *The Fellowship of the Ring*, Tolkien offers only the slightest explanation. Gandalf tells Frodo, "I can put it no plainer than by saying that Bilbo was *meant* to find the Ring, and *not* by its maker. In which case you also were *meant* to have it. And that may be an encouraging thought" (54–55). Here Tolkien uses italics to make sure we do not miss Gandalf's point. There is something very encouraging about the intentions of this invisible hand, because it clearly works for the benefit of Bilbo and the good peoples of Middle-earth.

Near the end of *The Fellowship of the Ring*, Boromir confronts Frodo and argues that the ring came to Bilbo and then to Frodo only by "unhappy chance" (390). It might just as well have been his, he asserts. While Boromir sees the agency behind the ring as nothing more than blind, random chance—like flipping a coin that is as likely to come up heads as it is tails—we are not meant to see it this way. Boromir's position on luck is not the author's, nor does Tolkien intend it to be our position.

Many Christians will find this concept of something greater than luck at work in Middle-earth to be akin to the way that God works in their own lives. Christian readers may see the Providence that surrounds, guides, and guards Bilbo to be very similar to the basic Christian doctrine of a loving Father who cares for his children. How exactly does this loving Father intervene in the world he has created? The answer, which lies at the foundations of Christian belief, is that he works in ways that are often mysterious though always compassionate, in ways we may better understand and better appreciate further along.

Tolkien expands on this idea at the Council of Elrond in *The Fellowship of the Ring*. There Elrond says to those assembled,

> What shall we do with the Ring, the least of rings, the trifle that Sauron fancies? . . . That is the purpose for which you are called hither. Called, I say, though I have not called you to me, strangers from distant lands. You have come and

are here met, in this very nick of time, by chance as it may seem. Yet it is not so. Believe rather that it is so ordered that we, who sit here, and none others, must now find counsel for the perils of the world. (236)

In the use of words like *purpose*, *called*, and *ordered*, words with distinctly Christian connotations, Tolkien continues to intimate that there is something or someone else at work in the seemingly coincidental events in Middle-earth, but the author refuses to be more explicit. As Patricia Spacks notes, "Over and over we find similar statements denying the existence of mere chance, insisting on some plan governing the activities of all" (60). Paul Kocher has identified an implied element of divine compassion in Elrond's statement, arguing: "Whoever did the calling was concerned for the West's welfare in the struggle against Sauron" (41). Kocher also points out "the care with which Elrond avoids giving the supreme being any of the traditional names for God," which is in keeping with Tolkien's stated purpose of omitting any references to anything like religion.

Why does Tolkien adopt this ongoing strategy of revealing and at the same time not revealing the Providence at work in Middle-earth? One reason is that he hopes to walk a fine line between courageous personal choices and divine care. As Tom Shippey suggests, "Too strong a flurry of angelic wings, too ready recourse to miracles or to Omnipotence" at these points would "diminish the stature of the characters" and "devalue their decisions and their courage" (*Road*,

151). If Bilbo were to suddenly believe that he was invulnerable to trolls, spiders, goblins, wargs, and a dragon because he is surrounded by omnipotent Divine Providence, the moral decisions he makes in *The Hobbit* would be largely meaningless.

Near the end of *The Fellowship of the Ring*, Galadriel offers her own version of Gandalf's earlier statements that there is an invisible hand at work for the good of Middle-earth and that this is an encouraging thought. The night before the company is to leave the safety of Lorien, Galadriel comforts them with these words: "Do not trouble your hearts overmuch with thought of the road tonight. Maybe the paths that you each shall tread are already laid before your feet, though you do not see them" (359).

Further Hints of an Unseen Hand

Readers still unconvinced about the presence of an unseen hand behind the apparent luck in *The Hobbit* can find further evidence in the prologue that Tolkien includes at the start of *The Fellowship of the Ring*. In the section titled "Of the Finding of the Ring," the narrator notes that the story told in *The Hobbit* would have earned little more than a short note in the history books "but for an 'accident' by the way" (11). Here the quotation marks Tolkien uses around the word *accident* point to a so-called accident, an event that we are meant to believe was anything but accidental.

In the prologue, Tolkien recounts how it happened that Bilbo became lost in the maze of tunnels under the Misty Mountains. And there, the narrator continues, as he groped blindly in the dark, Bilbo set his hand down on a ring that was lying on the floor of the tunnel, picked it up, and put it in his pocket. The narrator concludes, "It seemed then like mere luck" (11). In the word *then* Tolkien again says much about what has really brought about this unlikely event. Similarly, in the account of the riddling game with Gollum that Tolkien includes in the prologue, the narrator states that Bilbo won the game in the end "more by luck (as it seemed) than by wits" (11).

Tolkien makes a further comment about this other power that is at work behind the scenes in *The Hobbit*, but this time he tucks this information into appendix A in *The Return of the King*. There we learn about the events that led up to Gandalf's famous visit to Bilbo that early spring morning. We are told that Gandalf just happens to stop at Bree, where he just happens to run into Thorin. Thorin expresses surprise to see Gandalf but also gladness to have the chance to speak with him. Thorin explains to the wizard, "For you have often come into my thoughts of late, as if I were bidden to seek you. Indeed I should have done so, if I had known where to find you" (1052).

Readers are told that Gandalf looks at Thorin with a similar wonder and replies: "That is strange, Thorin Oakenshield. For I have thought of you also; and though I am on my way to the Shire, it was in my mind that is the way also to your halls" (1052). The narrator adds that the story is told elsewhere of the "strange plan" that Gandalf makes with the help of Thorin. The section ends with a conversation Gandalf has with Frodo and Gimli in Minas Tirith after the final overthrow of Sauron. Gandalf mentions with sadness the death of Dain, but comments that things could have been far worse. The threats from the Northern battle-front—dragon-fire, savage swords, and the overthrow of Rivendell—have all been averted. All because, as Gandalf explains, "I met Thorin Oakenshield one evening on the edge of spring in Bree. A chance meeting, as we say in Middle-earth" (1053).

In Gandalf's observation, Tolkien suggests that while those in Middle-earth might call the meeting with Thorin a chance occurrence, someone somewhere else would not use this word to describe how they happened to meet. With this incident as a backdrop, words found near the start of *The Hobbit* gain new resonance. In chapter 1 we are told that it was by "curious chance" that Gandalf came by as Bilbo happened to be standing at his door after breakfast smoking his pipe (5).

A Still, Small Voice

In "The Quest of Erebor"—an extra element Tolkien penned that can be found in *The Annotated Hobbit*—the author offers more details about the events that led up to Bilbo's adventure, including several additional examples of strange promptings. After telling of his meeting with Thrain in the dungeons of Dol Guldur and being given the map and key, which play such an important role in *The Hobbit*, Gandalf says, "By some warning of my heart I kept them always on me" (Anderson, 372). As it comes time for deciding who will go on the quest, Gandalf first explains, "I could not get Bilbo out of my mind." Though Gandalf confesses to the dwarves that choosing a hobbit to accompany them is an absurd notion, this urging becomes even stronger. Gandalf uses these words to describe it: "Suddenly I felt that I was indeed in hot earnest. This queer notion of mine was not a joke, it was *right*. It was desperately important that it should be carried out" (374).

The first of the dangerous encounters in *The Hobbit* occurs in chapter 2, when Bilbo and the dwarves come upon the trolls. In the end, they are saved only by Gandalf's providential return at the last moment. When asked what brought him back just in the nick of time, Gandalf explains that it was a chance encounter with two of Elrond's people who told him about the trolls and also, as he puts it, a "feeling" that he was wanted back (41). Again, many Christians would say that the way God or his Holy Spirit works in their own lives is often quite similar—through these very sort of mysterious feelings, proddings, stirrings, and seeming chance occurrences.

One of the most critical of the inexplicable, mysterious feelings in *The Hobbit* occurs in chapter 11, where Bilbo decides to wait all day in the grassy bay outside the stone door to the mountain. Readers are told he is prompted by a "queer feeling" that there is something he is waiting for (189). Without this strange feeling, Bilbo would not have been present on the last light of Durin's Day, and the company would never have been able to open the door.

A somewhat similar occurrence takes place in chapter 4 as the company takes shelter in the mountain cave. Tolkien's narrator states that "somehow" Bilbo is unable to sleep for a long while and that when he does finally drop off, his sleep is troubled by a strange dream about a crack in the wall that grows wider and wider (55). Suddenly in the dream Bilbo is falling down this crack, and this wakes him up. The hobbit then sees a real crack that the goblins have opened in the back wall of the cave and gives a loud yell. This allows Gandalf to remain uncaptured and so able to free them later.

What was the source of Bilbo's queer feeling about waiting for something and his strange dream about a crack? Tolkien never directly says, yet many Christians would say that promptings and interventions such as these described by Tolkien are a fundamental aspect of the Christian faith. While others would completely reject any notion of a supernatural being who intervenes in the world, many Christians would identify with this still, small voice that speaks in inexplicable ways. In this portrait of the hand of the Divine in Middle-earth, we see Tolkien's overall strategy of actually describing the real world as seen through Christian eyes.

In *The Fellowship of the Ring*, readers find other instances of strange promptings that are heeded with good results. When Gandalf tells Frodo about the growing unease he had about the ring during the years after Bilbo had returned with it to the Shire, he explains that he considered consulting Saruman, but each time "something" held him back (47). Had Gandalf not listened to this something, had he ignored the inner voice that warned against it and gone to Saruman with the story of Bilbo's ring, all would have been lost. A few pages later, in talking about Gollum, Gandalf uses the phrase "my heart tells me" as another way to describe this inner voice, stating, "My heart tells me that he has some part to play yet" (58).

Readers may best identify with the words that Sam uses to express this curious sense of intuition that transcends mere logic and ordinary feelings. The morning after meeting with Gildor and the band of elves in *The Fellowship of the Ring*, Sam tells Frodo that he feels differently about their quest. He explains: "I seem to see ahead, in a kind of way. I know we are going to take a very long road, into darkness; but I know I can't turn back. . . . I don't rightly know what I want: but I have something to do before the end, and it lies ahead, not in the Shire. I must see it through, sir, if you understand me" (85).

Sam's statement—"I seem to see ahead, in a kind of way"—echoes the observation found in 1 Corinthians 13:12: "Now we see through a glass, darkly."

The Effect Intentions Have on Outcomes

In *The Two Towers*, Tolkien has Gandalf explain to Aragorn the significance of having right intentions, no matter if in the end things do not play out according to plan. Commenting on Aragorn's choice to first devote time to Boromir's funeral and only afterward to pursue the orcs that took Merry and Pippin captive, Gandalf states, "Do not regret your choice in the valley of the Emyn Muil, nor call it a vain pursuit. You chose amid doubts *the path that seemed right: the choice was just, and it has been rewarded*" (489, emphasis added). Gandalf's point here is that intentions have significance in Middle-earth. Although Aragorn, Legolas, and Gimli arrive too late to rescue Merry and Pippin, something even better happens. Somehow, and in a way that is never explained, Providence rewards good intentions in Tolkien's fiction. If someone sets out to do the right thing, that aim will be recompensed. As David Mills observes, events in Middle-earth "work out for the good because the heroes do the right thing," and in this "some supervening power is clearly at work" (23).

In his book *Following Gandalf*, Matthew Dickerson notes that Tolkien's characters are responsible "only for their own choices and not for the outcome of those choices," and that many of these choices "result in a greater good than was imagined" (195). Dickerson points out that Gandalf does not say that Aragorn's choice was strategic, effective, or even wise, but rather that it was *right* and *just*. In fact, at one point in *The Two Towers*, Aragorn declares that all his choices "have gone amiss" (415). Providence is able to take right and just choices and reward them, making them, as Dickerson concludes, "bear fruit that may be unintended but that is good."

In *The Two Towers*, Gandalf sets out to round up Theoden's scattered forces at Helm's Deep. But what actually happens—the arrival of the treelike huorns who change certain defeat into victory—turns out to be even better than he had planned. Gandalf describes the outcome as "better than my design" (530). He does not mention the role Providence has played, but his words hint at it. He tells Theoden, "I see the wood as plainly as you do. But that is no deed of mine." In the expressions "no deed of mine" and "better than my design," readers can hear the implication of a deed and design belonging to someone else.

In *The Hobbit* we see this same pattern of an outside force rewarding good intentions—the same unseen hand that is behind the so-called luck—in two of Bilbo's most significant actions: his conversation with Smaug and his decision to give Bard the Arkenstone. In both these incidents, as William Green points out, Bilbo "does his best, his very brave best, and events providentially fall into place" (98).

After his conversation with Smaug in chapter 12, Bilbo regrets that in his riddling he referred to himself as Barrel-rider. Given this clue, the hobbit is sure the dragon will figure out they came from Lake-town and has a horrible feeling that Smaug will seek vengeance. Bilbo is correct in thinking that his choice to call himself Barrel-rider will cause Smaug to attack the residents of Lake-town. But Bilbo is mistaken in believing that the outcome of his well-intentioned mistake will be only negative. Bilbo's intentions were good, and in Smaug's attack on Lake-town, the dragon is brought down by Bard in a way that the hobbit could never have foreseen.

In chapter 18, Bilbo looks back on his foiled actions as a peacemaker and concludes, "You are a fool, Bilbo Baggins, and you made a great mess of that business with the stone; and there was a battle, in spite of all your efforts to buy peace and quiet" (259). Certainly Bilbo's intentions here are good as well. It is equally certain that these intentions do not come to pass as he had hoped. Thorin does not redeem the Arkenstone with Bilbo's share of the treasure, allowing the warring parties to part peacefully. However, Bilbo's plan delays the battle for twenty-four hours, as Bard gives Thorin until noon the next day to come up with the agreed-upon portion of the hoard. Because Dain receives news of Bilbo's action, he marches his dwarf troops throughout the night to arrive before the deadline, getting them there just in time to assist in the battle against the goblins and wargs.

The most significant illustration of how good intentions have an effect on outcomes in Middle-earth is seen in Bilbo's decision to spare Gollum. In the second chapter of *The Fellowship of the Ring*, Frodo disagrees with the choice Bilbo made under the Misty Mountains, and wishes that Bilbo had killed Gollum then and there when he had the chance. In the climactic scene on Mount Doom where Gollum attacks first Sam and then Frodo and takes back the ring, the wisdom of sparing Gollum is again briefly called into question. After Gollum and the ring perish in the Cracks of Doom, Gandalf might say not only to Bilbo but also to Frodo and Sam words similar to those he used with Aragorn: "Do not regret your choice to spare Gollum. You chose amid doubts *the path that seemed right: the choice was just, and it has been rewarded.*"

In fact, Gandalf does say something nearly like this. In *The Fellowship of the Ring*, in speaking to Frodo about Bilbo's intentions, the wizard claims that it was pity and mercy that stayed his hand, and that for these intentions Bilbo has been "well rewarded" (58).

If Providence can be seen in the effect that good intentions have on outcomes, what about evil intentions? If good intentions are in some mysterious way rewarded, in what respect might we say that evil intentions are punished in Middle-earth? In *The Return of the King*, Gandalf tells Pippin, "A traitor may betray himself and do good that he does not intend" (797). While Gandalf is speaking specifically about Gollum here, his words hold true for several other characters in *The Hobbit* and *The Lord of the Rings*.

In *The Two Towers*, Gandalf explains how Sauron's and Saruman's evil designs end up backfiring, stating, "So between them our enemies have contrived only to bring Merry and Pippin with marvelous speed, and in the nick of time, to Fangorn, where otherwise they would never have come at all!" (486). The two hobbits rouse the Ents of Fangorn, who turn the tide in the battle. Similarly in *The Hobbit* we could say that when the goblins capture Bilbo and the dwarves, they contrive to bring Bilbo to the exact right place deep below the mountain to find the ring where otherwise he would never have come at all.

We find another illustration of thwarted evil intentions near the end of *The Hobbit* when the arrival of the goblins and wargs works to unite those they fight in a way they never intended. In chapter 17, we learn that Dain and his dwarves have decided to take advantage of the hesitation of Bard and the Elvenking to strike first. Suddenly, without a signal, dwarf bows twang and their arrows begin to whistle. Had nothing else intervened, the goblins could have arrived at a later time and would have had an easy task of defeating whatever remnants were left. However, at that very moment, the vanguard of the goblins arrives, and with the coming of the goblin army all other quarrels are forgotten. This gives Gandalf the opportunity to call a meeting of the leaders who moments earlier faced each other as enemies. As the narrator concludes, so begins a battle "none had expected" (251).

Paul Kocher points out Tolkien's principle of "evil bringing forth good" (46), summing up the author's position this way: "Providence, therefore, not only permits evil to exist but weaves it inextricably into its purpose for Middle-earth. In the short term it may even allow evil to triumph. . . . Morning will come again and good will flourish no matter how complete the devastation wrought by evil seems" (48–49).

But what about the problem of free will? On the final page of *The Hobbit,* both Bilbo and Gandalf mention the "prophecies" about Lake-town's resurgence that have come true (272), and the use of the word *prophecies* suggests some predetermining power at work. If the unseen hand of Providence intervenes in the seemingly lucky events in

Middle-earth, rewarding good intentions and frustrating evil ones, does it mean that everything is actually playing out according to a fixed destiny? Kocher offers this cogent description of the way that the divine plan and the free will of those Gandalf offers assistance to each have a role in the eventual outcome:

> The future is the property of the One who plans it. Yet is it fixed in the sense that every link in the chain of its events is fore-ordained? It cannot be, because in his encounter with Gollum Bilbo's choice to kill or not to kill is genuinely free, and only after it has been made is it woven into the guiding scheme. . . . Human (or hobbitic or elvish or dwarfish or entish) free will coexists with a providential order and promotes this order, not frustrates it. (36)

One of Tolkien's most poignant observations about the importance of free will and the significance of the decisions we must make can be found in chapter 2 of *The Fellowship of the Ring,* in Gandalf's response to Frodo's wish that the Shadow had not reappeared during his time. "So do I," the wizard tells him, "and so do all who live to see such times. But that is not for them to decide. *All we have to decide is what to do with the time that is given*" (50, emphasis added).

As if to emphasize the free will that is such a critical part of Middle-earth, Tolkien has numerous paired characters in

The Hobbit who make opposite choices with opposite outcomes. Bilbo does not become like Gollum. Unlike Thorin, Dain proves to be generous with the dragon's treasure. The new Master of Lake-town chooses to govern very differently than the old one.

In *The Lord of the Rings*, Tolkien continues to call attention to personal free will with these pairings of opposite choices. Gandalf rejects the path that Saruman takes. Aragorn resists the temptation of the ring that his ancestor Isildur succumbed to. Faramir and Boromir take opposite paths in their encounters with Frodo. Theoden and Denethor make very different choices, which lead to very different final outcomes for each of them.

In the effect that intentions have upon outcomes in Middle-earth, the mysterious way that good intentions are somehow rewarded and evil intentions are somehow thwarted, many Christians will hear an echo of the fundamental Christian principle outlined in Romans 8:28: "And we know that all things work together for good to them that love God, to them who are the called according to his purpose."

In a letter to his son Christopher, Tolkien proposes that this notion that all things work together for good to them that love God is something we know more by faith than by sight. Tolkien explains: "All we do know . . . is that evil labors with vast power and perpetual success—in vain: preparing always only the soil for unexpected good to sprout in. So it is in general, and so it is in our own lives" (*Letters*, 76).

Strange Help

In chapter 10, Bilbo looks out over the landscape as he floats downriver on the raft of barrels. Soon the trees of Mirkwood thin out and come to an end, the lands open wide, and across the marshes the Lonely Mountain suddenly comes into view. As the hobbit listens to the raftmen discuss the disagreements about who should be taking care of the Forest River and its banks, he learns something even Gandalf did not know. In recent years the area has changed much. Earthquakes, great floods, and heavy rains have caused the bogs and marshes to swell over their borders, bringing the elf-road to a "doubtful and little used end" on the edge of the forest (172). "So you see," the narrator comments about the hobbit's river trip, "Bilbo had come in the end by the only road that was any good" (172).

Because of the changes, we are told Bilbo is very fortunate to have even made it to see the mountain. Had he and the dwarves stuck to the elf-road as they had planned, they would have been stranded on the edge of the swampland where all paths vanished and "many a rider and wanderer too, if they tried to find the lost ways across" (172). Yes, all those long days of imprisonment among the elves were dreary. Yes, his position perched atop the barrels is cold and unpleasant. Still, Bilbo concludes he has been "more lucky than he had guessed" (170). As we have seen, Bilbo's luck is really help from an unseen hand, so we could say that Bilbo has received more help than he had guessed. Admittedly it is a strange help, the kind that does not seem like help until long afterward.

In chapter 5 of *Prince Caspian*, we find Narnia is under the rule of the evil King Miraz, and the young Caspian has to flee for his life. His tutor, Doctor Cornelius, gives Queen Susan's magic horn to Caspian with these last-minute words: "It is said that whoever blows it shall have strange help—no one can say how strange" (62). When Caspian finally blows the horn, it does bring help, but not in the form anticipated. Caspian's forces were expecting that perhaps High King Peter and his mighty consorts would arrive. Peter and his siblings do arrive, but in the form of children, not as mighty warriors.

This *strange help* is, in fact, exactly the sort of assistance Bilbo has been receiving all throughout *The Hobbit*. The cheerless imprisonment among the elves and the wet, chilly night of barrel-riding certainly did not seem anything like help at the time. Yet now, in looking back, he sees it has brought him to the only road that would have sufficed. And this is not the first time that Bilbo has been the recipient of this kind of blessing in disguise. Falling off Dori's back during the escape from the goblins and being knocked unconscious certainly did not seem like help, yet without it he would never have found the ring. In a similar way, their encounter with the trolls did not seem like help, but without it Bilbo would not have had Sting, which he acquired from the trolls' booty, to use against the spiders when he needed it.

Perhaps the strangest form of strange help in *The Hobbit* comes in the form of no help at all. While there are a number of times that Bilbo wishes Gandalf were around, as any teacher knows, one of the best ways to help pupils is to allow them to face and solve problems on their own. In fact, facing these kinds of trials is part of what makes them who they are. And Tolkien, who was not only a teacher but also a father, understood this concept. After Bilbo kills the spider in chapter 8, Tolkien has his narrator explain that "somehow the killing of the giant spider, all alone by himself in the dark without the help of the wizard or the dwarves or of anyone else, made a great difference to Mr. Baggins" (141–42).

When Frodo wakes up at Rivendell in *The Fellowship of the Ring*, he finds Gandalf sitting near his bedside. One of the first things Frodo wants to know is where Gandalf has been during the perilous journey from the Shire. Gandalf replies that he was delayed and that this delay nearly caused their ruin. Despite this, he concludes, "It may have been better so" (214).

It may have been better that Gandalf was delayed, taken captive by Saruman and imprisoned in Orthanc for more than two months, finally escaping only with the help of Gwaihir the eagle?

It is not until more than forty pages later that Gandalf explains that because he was delayed and so was not with the rest of the company, he was able to draw off four of the Black Riders. "That helped a little," he explains at the Council of Elrond. "For there were only five, not nine, when your camp was attacked" (258). Perhaps, too, as Gandalf looks at the growth in courage and determination Frodo has gained from traveling on his own, this is another reason it may have been better so. Perhaps if Gandalf had not been delayed and had been with the hobbits all the way from the Shire, Frodo would not have become self-reliant enough to be able to declare, as he does at the Council of Elrond, that he is willing to take the ring to Mount Doom.

Christians are well acquainted with these sort of blessings in disguise in their own lives, this assistance that looks like help only long afterward. In fact, some might say that God specializes in this kind of strange help.

Some Have Found It Absurd

Not much is said in *The Hobbit* about who Gandalf is or where he has come from. In the opening chapter, the narrator confesses that he has heard only very little of all that there is to hear, but then goes on to add that wherever Gandalf goes, tales and adventures sprout up in a "most extraordinary" manner (5). Gandalf is not omnipotent. After he rescues the company from the goblins in chapter 4, we are told that although Gandalf can do a great deal for friends who are in a tight corner, he "could not do everything" (62). After the final battle, he is shown with his arm in a sling, and the narrator comments that even the wizard had not escaped without an injury. Like Elrond, Gandalf is knowledgeable but not omniscient. In chapter 4, the narrator explains that "even the good plans of wise wizards like Gandalf and of good friends like Elrond go astray sometimes" (53). As has been noted, in chapter 10 Bilbo discovers that conditions on the opposite side of Mirkwood have deteriorated since the last news that Gandalf had, and that the elf-road the wizard had earlier advised them to take is now impassable.

In the appendix B found at the end of *The Return of the King*, Tolkien offers a small window into Gandalf's extraordinary nature, telling us that the wizards were "messengers sent to contest the power of Sauron, and to unite all those who had the will to resist him" (1059). In *The Two Towers*, when Gandalf returns after his ordeal with the Balrog, he explains, "Naked I was sent back—for a brief time, until my task is done" (491).

Messengers sent to contest the power of Sauron. Naked I was sent back. Sent by whom? Neither omnipotent, omniscient, nor immortal, Gandalf is not divine himself, but only an emissary. While Tolkien does not make it explicit, we can conclude that whoever sent Gandalf is also behind the so-called luck in *The Hobbit*.

In *The Hobbit*, we see several instances of Gandalf's mission to contest Sauron, or the Necromancer as he is referred to, the first actually taking place a century before the story opens. In chapter 1 the wizard explains that he was on a dangerous mission in the dungeons of the Necromancer, a task with a purpose of finding things out, when he met Thorin's father, Thrain, and received the map and the key. At the end of chapter 7, when Gandalf leaves on an urgent errand to the south, it is to join forces with the White Council to drive Sauron from his fortress in Dol Guldur. If, as some suggest, Sauron may be behind the goblins and wargs' attack in the Battle of the Five Armies, then Gandalf, in his assistance during the battle, could be said to be opposing Sauron there also.

In *The Hobbit*, Gandalf refers to the mission he has been sent to Middle-earth to perform as his *business*. Early in chapter 1, Tolkien's narrator tells us that Gandalf has been almost forgotten by the residents of the Shire because he has been away on "business of his own" since they were young (5). Toward the end of the chapter, Gandalf explains that when he met Thorin's father, he was on "dangerous business" in the dungeons of the Necromancer (24). When he leaves Bilbo and the dwarves at the edge of Mirkwood in chapter 7, Gandalf explains he has "pressing business" away to the south (125). In chapter 1 of *The Fellowship of the Ring*, readers are told that while the residents of the Shire know Gandalf for his fireworks, his "real business" is much more dangerous and difficult (25). In *The Return of the King*, Gandalf uses a different word to describe his role in Middle-earth, telling Denethor, "I also am a steward" (742). While Denethor has been entrusted as the Steward of Gondor to preserve the realm until the return of the king, Gandalf is the steward of a much larger realm and of a far greater authority.

What is worth noting is the way that Gandalf and whoever sent him work together— both in *The Hobbit* and in *The Lord of the Rings*. It is the opposite of the way Sauron operates. In appendix B we learn that the wizards were forbidden to match Sauron's power with power or to seek to dominate elves or men—and we might also add hobbits and dwarves—by fear or force. We are also  told that Gandalf bears Narya, the Ring of Fire. In giving the ring to the wizard, Cirdan tells him that it is not to overpower, but to "rekindle" hearts (1060). In a letter Tolkien explains that the wizards were to limit their use of power in order that they could accomplish the task they were sent for: to "train, advise, instruct, arouse the hearts and minds of those threatened by Sauron to a resistance with their own strengths; and not just to do the job for them" (*Letters*, 202). And this is exactly what Gandalf does.

We see Gandalf encourage both Bilbo and Frodo to accept the adventure that they have been selected for, but never force or intimidate them. Gandalf never does for them what they need to do themselves. Tolkien has conveniently removed Gandalf from the scene when Bilbo chooses to go down the tunnel and face Smaug, and later when he chooses to give Bard the Arkenstone. The wizard is there to congratulate Bilbo for his daring actions as a peacemaker only afterward as the hobbit is about to return to the dwarves and accept the consequences of his decision.

Five years after the publication of *The Hobbit*, C. S. Lewis explored the issue of coercion and free will in *The Screwtape Letters*, a book he dedicated to Tolkien. Lewis, through Screwtape, describes the limited way in which Providence chooses to work, stating: "The Irresistible and the Indisputable are the two weapons which the very nature of His scheme forbids Him to use. . . . He cannot ravish. He can only woo" (39). Screwtape concludes that, given the Divine's insistence on voluntary cooperation, merely overriding a human will would be for him useless, because while Satan wants, in Screwtape's words, "cattle who can finally become food," God wants "servants who can finally become sons." Readers may hear an echo of these policies within *The Fellowship of the Ring* in Gandalf's words to Frodo describing Sauron's intentions. Gandalf explains that hobbits as "miserable slaves" would satisfy Sauron far more than hobbits who are "happy and free" (48).

Thomas Hibbs describes the distinction between the two powers, writing: "Tolkien manages to suggest the working of a higher, benevolent power, a providential orchestration of events. Unlike Sauron, whose attempt to see and control all is obvious to those involved in the cosmic war between good and evil, the hand of providence is neither clear nor compelling" (167). Hibbs concludes, "We will find very little direct evidence of the providential power at work in Middle-earth. What we find are suggestions, clues, and hints that enliven and deepen our appreciation of the mysterious way in which all things seem to work together for the good" (168).

In his essay "Christian Themes in Tolkien," Paul Pfotenhauer makes a similar point, writing, "Tolkien is saying that events are finally shaped by a Power that remains unseen, goes almost unnoticed, and sometimes uses the most unlikely persons as His agents" (14). In *The Two Towers* we find a clear example of how this unseen Power can use the most unlikely persons when Wormtongue throws the seeing-stone at Gandalf and the others gathered at the base of Orthanc. After Gandalf realizes what it is, what its loss will mean to Saruman, and how it might be used, he states that they could have found few treasures in Orthanc more precious than the one thing Wormtongue threw down. Gandalf concludes, "Strange are the turns of fortune!" (571).

Readers who do not see an invisible Power at work behind unlikely coincidences like this one may decide that the turns of fortune in Tolkien's fiction are simply too strange.

In the "Foreword to the Second Edition" of *The Fellowship of the Ring*, Tolkien acknowledges that some reviewers had found his work "boring, absurd, or co ntemptible," and then adds: "I have no cause to complain, since I have similar opinions of their works, or of the kinds of writing that they evidently prefer" (xiv). Certainly many modern critics would find the notion of a world where an unseen but loving hand rewards good intentions and thwarts evil ones—guiding but not dominating, wooing but not ravishing—to be absurd. Similarly, Christians find the idea of a world designed and guided by nothing more than blind chance and filled with rational beings who have no creator and no purpose, who simply live and then die without any meaning other than what they construct themselves, to be absurd.

What may seem the most absurd of all to non-Christians is why this powerful unseen hand of divinity does not simply obliterate Sauron and his minions. Why use men, elves, dwarves, and hobbits, who, in addition to being far less powerful, all have weaknesses and imperfections? Why use compassion, understanding, and mercy rather than power and might? Tolkien biographer Charles Moseley offers this summary of the foundations of Christianity, the essential convictions that were fundamental to Tolkien and his fiction and that many of his critics find so absurd:

Christianity . . . envisages a creator who, not simply a
watchmaker, loves his world, suffers in its sufferings, lives
in it, and sustains it in life. Christianity offers, too, . . . a
vision of history which is not meaningless or merely cyclic,
but purposive. . . . A mind really believing this must accept
that "Good" and "Evil" are not relative or subjective
terms . . . but represent a fundamental divide in the
Universe. . . . This sense of a damaged world, pointing
beyond itself . . . underlies all Tolkien's fiction and all his
writing about fiction. (10–11)

In a letter written to his son Christopher, Tolkien
observes that we humans are "placed so as to face (or to be
able to face) God" (*Letters*, 66). But at the same time,
Tolkien points out, God is also "behind us, supporting, nour-
ishing us" in ways that cannot be seen. In *The Hobbit*,
Tolkien gives us a glimpse of this unseen Divine Providence
that supports and nourishes with care and compassion.

"VERY GOOD FOR YOU": PURPOSE IN *THE HOBBIT*

The Chosen and Selected Burglar

As we have seen, Bilbo's adventures are brought about with a special kind of providential help. They also have a special kind of purpose.

In the opening chapter the narrator sums up the tale he is about to tell of how a Baggins had an adventure. Bilbo Baggins, we are told, "may have lost the neighbors' respect, but he gained—well, you will see whether he gained anything in the end" (4). In the final chapter, Tolkien has Gandalf observe, "You are not the hobbit that you were" (270). Clearly in the end Bilbo does gain something: he becomes the person he had the potential to be. All along, his adventure has had a greater purpose than merely reclaiming the dwarves' treasure.

Many of Tolkien's contemporaries, writers such as Sartre and Beckett, depicted a universe that seemed *purposeless*, one populated by people whose lives had no real meaning. By contrast, in *The Hobbit* we find a world charged with a special kind of purpose—one that is beneficial in a particular way for both the individual and the world he is a part of. This purpose is similar to the one that is a part of the foundations of the Christian faith.

In chapter 1, when Gandalf tells Thorin and the dwarves that Bilbo is the "chosen and selected" burglar (21), it is hard not to share the dwarves' doubts and disbelief. As someone accurately described by Gloin as looking "more like a grocer than a burglar" (18), Bilbo displays little in the beginning that suggests he will be an asset on the quest. His most defining characteristic at this point seems to be his excessive need for the comforts and safety found in his snug hobbit-hole— his warm fireplace and kettle, his cakes and fine waistcoats, and his pocket handkerchiefs. Even five chapters later, when the dwarves discover that Bilbo did not escape from the goblins with them, the consensus is still that he has been more trouble to them than use.

So why was Bilbo chosen? The answer, as we discover, is twofold. Bilbo has a greater potential that only Gandalf— and whoever has sent Gandalf—can see. This forms the basis for the entire story. The adventure is going to allow a part of

Bilbo to emerge that needs to emerge. Through it he will become the hobbit he was intended to be. We could say that the adventure will be the making of him. And at the same time, Bilbo has been chosen, not just because the adventure will do him good, but because he has something good to do for Middle-earth. The two purposes go hand in hand. Through the action of helping to save those around him, Bilbo will himself be saved, saved from a life bounded and surrounded by—as readers are shown—an inordinate need for predictability, safety, and comfort.

In chapter 1, when Gandalf first announces that he is looking for someone to share in an adventure he is planning, the hobbit replies that hobbits are plain quiet folk and have no use for adventures and that he cannot think what anybody sees in them. Although Bilbo and the quiet residents of Hobbiton have no use for adventures and see nothing in them, Gandalf does. So does whomever Gandalf is acting as emissary for. While the stated purpose of the adventure is to get the treasure from Smaug, it soon becomes clear that the adventure has a purpose that goes far beyond merely getting the dwarves' treasure back.

When Gandalf tells the disbelieving hobbit that he is going to send him on an adventure, the wizard promises, "Very good for you—and profitable too" (7). Exactly how will it be good for Bilbo, and in what way will it be profitable?

As it turns out, the adventure is actually *not* that profitable to Bilbo, not in the sense that he returns home with the rightful share of the treasure he was promised at the start.

Instead of a one-fourteenth portion of the enormous wealth of Smaug's hoard, in the end Bilbo brings home only two small chests, one with silver and one with gold, no more than can be carried by one strong pony. Although Bilbo and Gandalf also retrieve the trolls' plunder they had buried near the start of the journey, neither is this a large sum. The relatively modest amount Bilbo has left over after buying back his own possessions is largely spent in presents. In *The Fellowship of the Ring*, when Strider and the hobbits come upon the stone marking where the treasure acquired by the trolls was hidden, Merry will wonder how much of Bilbo's share remains. Frodo will reply that Bilbo gave it all away, as he felt it was not really his since it came from robbers.

So if Bilbo's adventure, in Gandalf's words, is in some way profitable for the hobbit, it is profitable only in terms of acquiring a very different kind of treasure, which is exactly Tolkien's point. Tolkien hints at this deeper meaning in the mark Gandalf puts on Bilbo's door. While typically interpreted to mean "burglar," as Gloin notes, it can also mean "expert treasure-hunter" (18). It could be argued that Bilbo, like his door, is marked for something special. Bilbo's adventure is, as Gandalf says, very good for the hobbit, but not in a financial way. The real treasure he brings home is the kind that will never rust and cannot be stolen by thieves.

We find a similar idea in *The Silver Chair* and in many of the other Chronicles of Narnia. In *The Silver Chair*, C. S. Lewis sends his two protagonists, Jill and Eustace, on a quest with a Marsh-wiggle named Puddleglum, who, on the surface, seems to fit his name, as he lives near a pond and appears quite gloomy. At one point Eustace suggests that since the Marsh-wiggle seems to feel their quest is hopeless, he should just stay behind. Puddleglum responds, "I'm not going to lose an opportunity like this. It will do me good" (75). In fact, the adventure does good for all three characters.

Tolkien makes this same point near the end of *The Return of the King* when the hobbits learn that all is not well back home. Gandalf announces that he will not be coming with them and they must set the Shire in order themselves. He explains that this is what they have been trained for, adding, "You are grown up now" (974). At the end of the next chapter, Saruman comments on the change in Frodo, and his eyes take on a look of wonder. "You have grown, Halfling," he declares. "Yes, you have grown very much" (996).

Does Bilbo have any sense that the adventure will, as Gandalf says, be good for him? Tolkien does not say much to directly answer this question but does provide one very curious hint. At the end of chapter 6, Bilbo has a dream as he and the dwarves sleep high up on the eagles' rock shelf after being rescued from the goblins and wargs. In the dream, Bilbo is back at Bag-End wandering through each of the rooms, looking for "something that he could not find nor remember what it looked like" (102). The implication seems to be that by this point partway through the adventure, Bilbo has the sense—somewhere deep down inside of him—that he is missing something. He cannot quite put his finger on this something, but readers know what it is. What is more, Bilbo also has a growing sense that this thing he is missing cannot be found at home. Again readers can see a bit further than Bilbo and know that this missing element, Bilbo's realization of his full potential, will be found only in the adventure that lies ahead of him.

"And That Means Comfort"

In chapter 3 of *The Fellowship of the Ring*, Frodo tells Gandalf, "Bilbo went to find a treasure, . . . I go to lose one" (65). It turns out that part of the treasure Bilbo goes to find in *The Hobbit* is, as the narrator calls it, his "Took side," something that we are told "only waited for a chance to come out" (5). But it can also be argued that Bilbo goes on an adventure to lose something as well. Bilbo goes to lose what might be called his anti–Took side, the side that is a slave to all the comforts of home.

Tolkien's famous opening line—*In a hole in the ground there lived a hobbit*—is followed by this further description: "Not a nasty, dirty, wet hole, filled with the ends of worms and an oozy smell, nor yet a dry, bare, sandy hole with nothing in it to sit down on or to eat: it was a hobbit-hole, and that means comfort" (3). On this same page we also learn that the Bagginses are considered very respectable, not only due to their wealth but also because they never have any adventures or do anything unexpected. When Gandalf tells Bilbo he is looking for someone to share in an adventure, the hobbit's immediate reaction is "Nasty disturbing uncomfortable things! Make you late for dinner!" (6). In Bilbo's response about not being disturbed or uncomfortable, and about being on time for dinner, we learn a great deal about what is most important to him at the start of the story.

If at the start Bilbo's defining values are comfort and predictability, it takes a long time for him to be completely freed from them. Even though we are told in the middle of chapter 1 that "the Took side had won" and that Bilbo is now ready to go without bed and breakfast if he might be thought fierce (18), he will need the rest of the book for his Took side to come out fully. Again and again, readers are reminded of how Bilbo longs to return to his formerly comfortable and safe life.

In chapter 2, as they leave the familiar countryside and the weather turns cold, gloomy, and wet, Bilbo exclaims to himself, "Bother burgling and everything to do with it!" and wishes he were back at home warm and dry (30). In chapter 3, when Bilbo has his first glimpse of the great mountains they must cross, his thoughts quickly turn to his comfortable chair in front of the fire and to his kettle singing on it. The narrator concludes, "Not for the last time!" (43), reminding readers again that overcoming his excessive need for comfort and safety will be a long, gradual process for Bilbo. A chapter later, as they begin the difficult climb, Bilbo gazes back toward home with its "safe and comfortable things" (52). After their capture, as he is being bounced along on Bombur's back beneath the Misty Mountains with the goblins in hot pursuit, Bilbo exclaims, "O why did I ever leave my hobbit-hole!" (62). Even as late as chapter 8, we find Bilbo still thinking of his distant hobbit-hole and especially its beautiful pantries.

One of the turning points in Bilbo's growth occurs in chapter 5 when he kills the spider. There Tolkien's narrator tells us, "He felt a different person, and much fiercer and bolder *in spite of an empty stomach*" (142, emphasis added). In the book's final chapter, we find a very different Bilbo than we saw at the start, one who tells the dying Thorin, "I am glad that I have shared in your perils" (258), making it clear that he has at last come to a point where he no longer wishes he could have stayed home. Though Bilbo still acknowledges the dangers and difficulties they have come through as perils, he no longer sees them as a torment but as a privilege, and the opportunity to share in them as having been "more than any Baggins deserves." In the end, it is clear to readers that Bilbo has been invited by Gandalf to leave the comfort, safety, and predictability of his former life in order that he may grow into something greater, into the hobbit he was meant to be, someone he would never have become if he had stayed in his pleasant and secure home.

In any story about a character's growth, readers must always be convinced that the character has potential for the change we witness. Near the middle of chapter 1, Tolkien offers a glimpse of Bilbo both as he is at the start of the story and also of the hobbit he will become. Dwalin, the first guest to appear, is already on his third cake when suddenly Balin shows up. At this point, the narrator tells us that Bilbo is briefly overwhelmed by a terrible thought. What is it that has troubled him so terribly? Bilbo is upset that the cakes might run short and that he, as host, may have to do without. This is just the sort of small-minded concern that would preoccupy Bilbo at this point, and so is an integral part of his character-ization. But Tolkien inserts another statement that also reveals a great deal about the hobbit. Readers are further told that Bilbo knows his "duty" and will stick to it no matter how painful (9). Although Bilbo's devotion to duty here involves nothing more than forgoing another cake, later, when the costs are much higher, his commitment to what he perceives as his responsibility will not diminish. In chapter

6—the next time Tolkien uses the word *duty*—Bilbo will decide that it is his duty to return to the "horrible, horrible tunnels" in order to look for his friends (84).

Tolkien highlights one change in Bilbo by bookending the story with the hobbit receiving unexpected guests. In chapter 1, the narrator states that Bilbo likes visitors but prefers the predictability of being able to invite them himself. When Gandalf and Balin show up unannounced and uninvited in the final chapter, Bilbo receives them warmly, even though they interrupt the writing of his memoirs.

Two more specific concerns preoccupy Bilbo at the story's start and thus, as he leaves them behind, become indicators of his growth and of the good the adventure does him. In the song they create in chapter 1 to mock the hobbit's inordinate preoccupation with his possessions, the dwarves sing, "Chip the glasses and crack the plates! . . . That's what Bilbo Baggins hates" (12). And, in fact, chipped glasses and cracked plates are exactly the kind of petty concerns that are the hobbit's biggest worries at this point.

Another trivial thing that Bilbo hates, as we learn in chapter 2, is being without a pocket handkerchief. Dwalin accurately points out to Bilbo that he will learn to manage without pocket handkerchiefs and a good many other things before they are through. This issue is revisited in chapter 12 when Bilbo must go down the tunnel to face Smaug the first time. There Tolkien makes it clear what good the adventure has done Bilbo. Although he is trembling with fear, his face is set and grim. Readers are told, "Already he was a very different hobbit from the one that had run out without a pocket handkerchief from Bag-End long ago. He had not had a pocket handkerchief for ages" (192). One clear purpose the adventure has for Bilbo, one way it is good for him, is to free him from the trifling concerns that threatened to dominate and define him.

Enemies—Internal and External

While Bilbo and the dwarves together confront a host of enemies on their journey—among them trolls, goblins, spiders, and wargs—there are two antagonists Bilbo must face on his own. In chapter 5, while he is separated from the group in the tunnels below the Misty Mountains, Bilbo encounters Gollum. Then later, in chapter 12, he must go alone down the tunnel to Smaug's lair. We could say that another enemy Bilbo must face alone is the enemy within—his own inner temptations. Gollum and Smaug can be seen to represent the dark side of Bilbo's personality, so it is significant that both encounters take place deep belowground in subterranean darkness. In overcoming these enemies, Bilbo can also be seen to overcome his own deep-seated flaws.

Gollum comes from the clan that produced the Stoor family of hobbits, and as Gandalf explains in chapter 2 of

The Fellowship of the Ring, Bilbo and Gollum share a kinship. Both characters live underground. Both like the riddling game. Gollum, as Gandalf tells Frodo, came from a family of high repute, which, like Bilbo's, was wealthy and had a strong matriarchal figure. Both characters lose the reputations their families had, though in quite opposite ways. Both are living alone without close connections to others. In fact, Gollum has become completely cut off from all society and a vicious law unto himself.

Perhaps the most significant similarity between the two is that each is described as possessing two warring natures. Gollum's wicked side has nearly replaced his Smeagol side, although as Gandalf tells Frodo, the miserable creature is not wholly ruined. There is still a small part of his good side that may yet be saved. Later Sam will refer to these two sides of Gollum as Slinker and Stinker.

We have seen that at the story's start, Bilbo was repressing his Took side. Now will Bilbo be like Gollum and give in to an even darker side? One of Bilbo's biggest decisions about what kind of a person he will become takes place, significantly, as Gollum stands before him blocking the escape from the goblin kingdom below the Misty Mountains. Bilbo initially thinks he should kill the foul creature and put its horrible eyes out. Bilbo has literally been following in Gollum's footsteps up the tunnel. Now he must decide if he will further follow Gollum by reacting with violence and, in this sense, become like him.

A thought from Bilbo's better side takes over. A "sudden understanding" wells up in him (80), and Bilbo decides, at risk to himself, to spare Gollum's life and to simply try to leap over him. This decision has great importance for Bilbo and for Middle-earth as well, for if Gollum had not been spared, the ring might never have been destroyed. Fleming Rutledge has written that the thought comes to Bilbo "There but for the grace of God go I"—and that this empathy becomes "the source of the new courage that propels him out of the tunnel into safety" (28). Rutledge concludes, "It can't be stated too strongly. This brief passage in *The Hobbit* lays out the theological foundation for the climax of *The Lord of the Rings*." As Tolkien biographers Ivor and Deborah Rogers point out, it can be argued that "the War of the Ring was won" under the Misty Mountains through Bilbo's decision to act with pity and mercy (69).

As Bilbo races down the tunnel toward freedom, leaving his shrieking foe behind, the narrator of *The Hobbit* reports that "Gollum was defeated" (80). But Bilbo is not done confronting his shadow side. In chapter 1 of *The Fellowship of the Ring*, Bilbo will, like Gollum, begin a journey on his birthday. But while Gollum acquired the ring on his birthday, Bilbo gives it away—though not without difficulty. At one point in the struggle, he uses Gollum's own words, telling Gandalf, "It is mine, I tell you. My own. My precious" (33). In a similar scene several chapters later, after Frodo reaches Rivendell with the ring, Bilbo will again briefly battle his dark side as he appears to confront Frodo in a form much like Gollum, as a "little wrinkled creature with a hungry face and bony groping hands" (226).

Despite these later struggles, in his confrontation and victory over Gollum beneath the Misty Mountains, Bilbo could be said to face and defeat his own strong tendency to prefer isolation over community. Bilbo's act of compassion here is exactly that, in the sense that compassion comes from root words meaning to bear or suffer with someone. In sparing Gollum, Bilbo both sees and accepts their underlying kinship. In the final chapter of *The Hobbit* we are told that rather than becoming old, lonely, and isolated like Gollum, Bilbo remains an elf-friend and has the honor of dwarves and wizards, and "all such folk as ever passed that way" (271).

In our last view of Gollum in *The Hobbit*, we see him hissing and cursing, alone in the tunnels below the Misty Mountains. The narrator tells readers that Gollum has lost his prey and also the "only thing he had ever cared for, his precious" (80). In contrast, in our last view of Bilbo at the end of *The Hobbit*, we see him talking, laughing, and sharing a pipe with the two closest friends from his journey. At the end of *The Lord of the Rings*, we find a similar contrast as Gollum falls alone into the Cracks of Doom, while Bilbo journeys with his companions over the sea to the Uttermost West.

The other antagonist that Bilbo faces alone and that also may be said to represent his shadow side or darker aspects that must be overcome is Smaug. Again, Tolkien sets up parallels to suggest a tie between the two. Again, both characters enjoy riddles. Again, as with Gollum, both creatures live underground: Smaug with his hoard of treasure; Bilbo with his paneled walls, tiled and carpeted floors, polished chairs, and entire rooms devoted to clothes. In the first description of them we are given, we see each in his respective home, blowing out wisps of smoke. Tolkien makes the association even clearer as Bilbo and Smaug share a fondness for ornamental waistcoats. They both have prescient dreams about danger—Bilbo in the cave in the Misty Mountains, Smaug in his lair under the Lonely Mountain. And each has his possessions distributed among his neighbors after his death—Smaug's death is literal, Bilbo's is presumed. In the opening paragraph of *The Fellowship of the Ring*, readers are told that Bilbo's neighbors mistakenly believe Bag-End is full of tunnels filled with treasure, much like Smaug's lair under the Lonely Mountain.

The connection between Bilbo's confrontation with Smaug and his confrontation with his inner enemy is most direct as Bilbo pauses in the tunnel before his first encounter with the dragon. Tolkien tells that he "fought the real battle in the tunnel alone," and that going forward despite his fears was the bravest thing the hobbit ever did (193). At this point it is obvious that the adventure has been good for Bilbo, bringing him a long way from his former self, who in chapter 1 shook like melting jelly at the mere mention of danger.

At the start of the story, Bilbo is at risk of becoming, like Smaug, inordinately fond of his own little hoard of his dishes, plates, and his pocket handkerchiefs. He is also in danger of becoming too attached to his life of self-governed solitude where he lives alone under the hill, touching no one and letting no one touch him. If Bilbo goes on a journey to save part of Middle-earth, in doing so he himself is saved from the prison house of a lesser life—the kind of life lived by Gollum and Smaug.

"Very Good for You" in a Distinctly Christian Sense

As has been mentioned, in chapter 1 the narrator tells us that Bilbo's adventure may have lost him his neighbors' respect, but concludes, "He gained—well, you will see whether he gained anything in the end" (4). In the end we see that Bilbo has gained something. His adventure has been very good for him in a distinctly Christian sense.

What exactly has Bilbo gained?

In chapter 1, Gandalf tells the dwarves that he selected Bilbo in part because no warrior was available. "In this neighborhood," the wizard explains, "heroes are scarce, or simply not to be found. Swords are mostly blunt, and axes are used for trees" (21). In a different type of story, over the course of the adventure Bilbo would have been transformed into the warrior that was missing. Through his experiences, we would have seen him gaining skill with Sting. And when he puts on his fabulous mithril coat in the end, he would have emerged as a conventional hero like Bard the Bowman, in the hobbit's case perhaps as Baggins the Blademan. In a different type of story, Bilbo would have been the one to kill Smaug, not Bard. In this other kind of story, it would have been Bilbo, not Beorn, who led the final charge, rescued Thorin's body, and defeated Bolg.

But this is not the tale Tolkien wants to tell.

Thorin's dying words offer a portrait of the Bilbo we find at the story's end. Thorin tells the hobbit there is more "good" in him than he knows, and courage and wisdom "blended in measure" (258–59). Bilbo's goodness and wisdom have been, in contrast to Thorin, to recognize what is of real value in the world and what is not. Bilbo's courage—which in a secondary way has been the conventional kind that many protagonists, particularly small ones, acquire through an adventure—appears primarily as a particularly Christian version of this virtue. The fact that Bilbo's courage and wisdom are, as Thorin suggests, blended in measure implies that either virtue without the other would be lacking a necessary component.

Bilbo Baggins, the former shrieker who at the mere mention of danger needed to be taken out and laid on his drawing-room sofa, in the end finds that he has the courage to face a mighty dragon all by himself, not once but twice. Just as impressive a show of what we typically think of as courage can be found earlier at the start of chapter 6, where Bilbo, having barely escaped the terror of Gollum and the goblins, worries that Gandalf and the dwarves are still inside. He wonders, now that he has the magic ring, whether he ought to go back and look for them. At just the moment that Bilbo decides he will go back, he hears their voices ahead of him along the path. In each of these cases, Bilbo's sense of obligation to others overcomes his fear of menacing monsters.

Although Bilbo acquires a sword in chapter 2, and near the story's end a helmet and chain mail, except for a brief time when he uses Sting against the spiders, he never becomes a warrior. "I expect I look rather absurd," the hobbit observes as he puts on the battle gear in chapter 13 (215). During the Battle of Five Armies, he chooses to stand on Ravenhill with the elves, but it will not be his part, as Frodo will later say in *The Return of the King*, to strike any blow again. As he looks on and fears what the outcome will be, Bilbo reflects that in the songs of battles he had heard, even defeat can be glorious. In reality, the hobbit decides there is nothing glorious about armed conflict, but rather it seems "very uncomfortable, not to say distressing," and he wishes he were "well out of it" (255), definitely not the sort of thing a warrior would say before the story's final conflict.

As if to underscore the fact that Bilbo's valor is not primarily the physical courage of a warrior, Tolkien has the hobbit get knocked unconscious and play no part in the climactic battle scene. Bilbo's view of warfare remains unchanged when he comes to in chapter 18 and discovers to his great surprise that the goblin army has been defeated. "Victory after all," he observes. "Well, it seems a very gloomy business" (257).

Even more significant than the measure of conventional courage he acquires is the hobbit's display of moral courage, a different form of bravery that his other deeds prepare him for.

Bilbo's first great display of moral courage is as a mercy-giver. When Gollum stops in the tunnel and stands between Bilbo and the opening to the outside, the hobbit becomes desperate. Bilbo thinks to himself that he "must get away, out of this horrible darkness" (80). "He must fight." But then, although it might be safer to kill Gollum, Bilbo decides it would not be right. Understanding and sympathy fill him. Then, "as if lifted by a new strength"—not the might of a conventional hero but a moral strength that seems to come from a source outside him—he leaps over Gollum rather than slaying him.

Bilbo's second great display of moral courage is as a peacemaker. While Thorin had told him that he might pick and choose his own share, when Bilbo discovers the Arkenstone in chapter 13 and secretly conceals it in his pocket, he knows that Thorin had not intended to include the gem in his offer. In chapter 16—a chapter whose title, "A Thief in the Night," has strong biblical overtones—Bilbo decides he must intervene in the growing conflict between dwarves, men, and elves. Though it will certainly mean facing the wrath of Thorin, the hobbit offers to give up his own share of the treasure, as contained in the Arkenstone. While there is little or no physical danger involved, it takes great moral courage for the hobbit to go alone with his offer to the opposing camp. It takes even more courage to return to Thorin and company and face the repercussions of his deed, but again Bilbo does this not because it is safe or expedient but because it is right. As he explains, "I don't think I ought to leave my friends like this, after all we have gone through together" (244).

Recognizing Bilbo's bravery in delivering the Arkenstone to Bard as even more extraordinary than the kind demonstrated on the battlefield, the Elvenking tells the hobbit he is "more worthy to wear the armor of elf-princes than many that have looked more comely in it" (244). Richard Purtill points out:

> The kind of courage exhibited by Bilbo in this incident is not the usual heroism of the folktales. He has to make a lonely moral decision as to rights and wrongs in a complex situation, devise a plan with no help or support from those who should be his friends, and carry it out alone. His return to face the rage of the Dwarves shows another kind of courage, exhibiting a sense of honor and obligation. . . . For all his pretense sometimes to be "businesslike" and "sensible," friendship is not a business matter for Bilbo: for him friendship involves giving even if you do not receive. The true word for what he calls friendship is love. (*Myth*, 66)

Another way to evaluate the purpose behind Bilbo's adventure and what Bilbo has gained in the end is to note what he has not become. Without the adventure, Bilbo risked becoming isolated in his comfortable hole under the hill, in this sense becoming somewhat like Gollum and Smaug. But most of all Bilbo risked becoming like his closest relatives, the Sackville-Bagginses, whose greed to have his elegant home and his other possessions is their defining quality, even causing them to deny that the returned Bilbo is genuine. Though his cousins are unable to give back the silver spoons they have taken from Bag-End, Bilbo is able to hand the Arkenstone over to Bard knowing it might be the means to bring peace.

Tolkien revisits the issue of the stolen spoons in the opening chapter of *The Fellowship of the Ring*. When Bilbo disappears from the Shire after his birthday party, he leaves an entire case of silver spoons labeled for Lobelia Sackville-Baggins. The narrator reports, "Bilbo believed that she had acquired a good many of his spoons, while he was away on his former journey" (37). Lobelia takes the point of Bilbo's gift. She also takes the spoons. She then insists on seeing Bilbo's will, which names Frodo as heir.

"Foiled again!" says Lobelia's husband, Otho, after they find that in correct hobbit fashion the will has been properly signed in red ink by seven witnesses (38). "And after waiting *sixty* years. Spoons? Fiddlesticks!"

In the last part of *The Return of the King*, Tolkien brings the story of the Sackville-Bagginses and the greed that consumes them to a conclusion. There Lobelia's son, Lotho, becomes hungry for more and more wealth—like the Master of Lake-town—and in the end is murdered by Wormtongue. By contrast, Lobelia reverses her earlier inclinations and gives Bag-End back to Frodo and in her will donates her estate to help the homeless.

An Abundant Life

In the final chapter of *The Hobbit*, our diminutive hero returns home only to find that the effects of the late Bilbo Baggins of Bag-End are being sold at auction. There is something fitting in the fact that Bilbo has been presumed dead, for his cyclic there-and-back journey represents a metaphorical death to an old way of living and a rebirth to a new kind of life, one that is richer, more deeply lived, and more abundant. This abundant life is the real wealth our expert treasure seeker has returned home with.

While a simplistic view of Bilbo's growth sees him as initially in bondage to his comfortable hobbit-hole and the pleasures it holds and at the end sees him as rejecting these things for a higher, less-material kind of existence, a careful reading shows a more nuanced transformation. To paraphrase the words of Tolkien's opening paragraph, we could say that Bilbo does *not* come home to live in a dry, bare, sandy hole with nothing in it to eat or sit down on. If anything, Bilbo's hobbit-hole is even more comfortable at the end than it was at the start. The Bilbo who welcomes Gandalf in the final chapter is not wholly different from the Bilbo who invites the wizard to join him on the porch for a pipe in chapter 1. He still looks more like a grocer than a burglar.

Earlier it was noted that Bilbo has two warring sides. Over the course of the adventure his Baggins side has not been so much conquered as redeemed. At the end we find a Bilbo who is in proper balance. His Took side and his Baggins side are, to use Thorin's final words, blended in measure. All the things that the Baggins in him loved and took delight in are loved even more once they have been put in their proper place.

With this in mind, we can find many defining things about Bilbo that do not change in the end, but actually become even more characteristic of him. Much to his dismay, Bilbo has to run off in chapter 1 without his pocket handkerchief, but Tolkien has him return home with an even nicer one, which is borrowed from Elrond and is made of red silk. In the first chapter we are told Bilbo has whole rooms devoted to clothes. In the final chapter, when Gandalf and Balin come to visit, they find Bilbo wearing a gold-buttoned waistcoat that is even more extensive than his previous one, which had brass buttons. When Bilbo stands up to make his farewell speech in the first chapter of *The Fellowship of the Ring*, he is described as wearing a waistcoat that not only is gold-buttoned but is also made of embroidered silk.

Bilbo is even fonder of his tea after he comes home—Tolkien tells us the sound of the kettle on his hearth is even more musical than before. The same could be said for Bilbo's love of his pipe and smoke rings. Tolkien ends *The Hobbit* with Bilbo's laughter as he passes Gandalf the tobacco jar so they may share a pipe together.

It is also clear that Bilbo continues to be very fond of his meals after his return. At the start of *The Fellowship of the Ring*, the narrator explains that the Sackville-Bagginses decide to attend his birthday party, in part because Bilbo has been "specializing in food" for years and his table has acquired a "high reputation" (28). The same point could be made about Bilbo's love of flowers. In chapter 1 of *The Hobbit*, we are told how fond he is of flowers. At the start of *The Fellowship of the Ring*, Gandalf comments on how bright Bilbo's garden looks with its snapdragons, sunflowers, and nasturtians, and the hobbit replies, "Yes, I am very fond of it" (25).

Bilbo's abundant new life is not confined to comforts. In chapter 1 we find Bilbo's colorful description of Gandalf's fireworks, followed by the narrator's comment that Bilbo is "not quite so prosy as he liked to believe" (7), indicating that even initially Bilbo has a proclivity toward poetry and figurative speech, though it is not very developed. On the way home, as Bilbo comes to a rise where he has the first sight of his own hill, he stops suddenly and breaks into fine lyrics that he composes on the spot, creating a song that extols the green meadows, trees, and hills he has long known. Tolkien has Gandalf remark on this increased poetic ability as well as the greater sensitivity to beauty that Bilbo displays. "My dear

Bilbo!" the wizard exclaims. "Something is the matter with you! You are not the hobbit that you were" (270). To further underscore this point, in *The Fellowship of the Ring*, when Frodo finds Bilbo at Rivendell, Tolkien places their reunion in the Hall of Fire, where Bilbo is making up a new song that he subsequently performs.

In *The Fellowship of the Ring*, Tolkien has Galadriel make this prediction to Gimli: "Your hands shall flow with gold, and yet over you gold shall have no dominion" (367). A similar observation could be made about Bilbo. He is not called to renounce his luxurious waistcoats, his lovely dishes, his cakes, pocket handkerchiefs, four o'clock tea, smoke rings, or any of the other things he has loved. When they are put in their proper place, one that does not dominate him, Bilbo is not called to forgo any of the pleasures of life, but to enjoy them even more fully and, in doing so, to live even more abundantly. This is a principle that many Christians will recognize as holding true in their own lives.

In Thorin's final words to Bilbo, he tells the hobbit, "If more of us valued food and cheer and song above hoarded gold, it would be a merrier world" (259). Throughout *The Hobbit* and *The Lord of the Rings* as well, Tolkien suggests again and again that right living involves a certain stance or attitude toward the things of creation, one of great delight but not slavish adoration.

Great delight but not slavish adoration—both parts of Tolkien's formula are equally important.

Tolkien's characters are intended to enjoy the comforts and pleasures given them but must be able to give them up if a greater need calls. In *The Two Towers*, when Pippin questions his decision to leave his beautiful Elven brooch on the side of the trail as a sign, Aragorn assures him he did rightly, stating, "One who cannot cast away a treasure at need is in fetters" (550). In *The Hobbit*, we could say that Bilbo's inner journey is a quest to be free of the fetters that bind him to the comforts of his hobbit-hole. Tolkien is not saying through Aragorn that we are to renounce all material goods, but that if we are unable to cast away a treasure even *if need demands*, then our possessions are possessing us.

In his fiction as well as his own life—one marked by an abundance of laughter shared with good friends and many a shared pipe and pint, Tolkien demonstrated his belief that all created things are good in themselves and meant to be enjoyed. This right and good enjoyment of earthly pleasures becomes a problem only through excessive attachment to them.

Tolkien would have encountered this idea of appropriate and excessive attachment—of ordinate and inordinate desires—in Saint Augustine. It was a concept that Tolkien embraced, as did Lewis, who discusses it in his *Letters to Malcolm*. There Lewis observes, "Our deepest concern should be for the first things, and our next deepest for second things, and so on down to zero—to total absence of concern for things that are not really good, nor means to good at all" (22). In a letter to Dom Bede Griffiths, Lewis argues, "Put first things first and we get second things thrown in: put second things first and we lose *both* first and second things" (*Collected Letters*, 111).

It is not just gold and cakes that Bilbo learns to value appropriately. There is one further item that Bilbo shows an excessive attachment to early in the story: his reputation among his neighbors. In chapter 1, when Thorin refers to him as *audacious* and as a *fellow-conspirator*, two terms the other residents of Hobbiton would never have approved of, we are told that Bilbo becomes so flummoxed he cannot speak. From the start, the narrator makes it clear that through the adventure Bilbo will lose his neighbors' respect. What is more important is that Bilbo will also lose his need for this kind of respect. In the final chapter, we are told that except for his nieces and nephews on his Took side, all of the hobbits in the neighborhood think Bilbo strange. The narrator concludes, "I am sorry to say he did not mind" (271), but we are meant to think that he is not sorry at all—and neither is Bilbo.

At the start of *The Fellowship of the Ring*, Tolkien tells us something important about how Bilbo no longer has a need for the superficial respect of his upper-crust neighbors. The narrator reports that in the years following his return, Bilbo came to have many admirers, but these admirers came from only "poor and unimportant families" (21). One of these poor and so-called unimportant families that Bilbo befriends is headed by Hamfast Gamgee, a humble local gardener whose specialty is growing potatoes. Several chapters later, after reciting a poem about the Elven-king Gil-galad, the young Sam Gamgee will reveal, "I learned it from Mr. Bilbo when I was a lad. . . . It was Mr. Bilbo as taught me my letters" (181).

On the final page of *The Hobbit*, Bilbo learns from Balin that the old Master of Lake-town has come to a bad end. After fleeing with the gold Bard had given him to help the townspeople, the former master is soon deserted by his attendants and dies alone of starvation. By contrast we see Bilbo well-fed and surrounded by the two closest companions from his trip. The difference is that while Bilbo possesses gold and all it brings, this gold—with its comforts and pleasures—does not possess Bilbo. And this has been one purpose for Bilbo's adventure.

"When God made the world he declared it good, and even in its fallen state, it offers an abundance of good and proper pleasures," writer and scholar Jonathan Rogers observes (131). "A properly Christian view of things requires more than a right relationship to the things of heaven," Rogers concludes. "It requires a right relationship to the things of earth too." One of the treasures Bilbo finds on his journey is this right relationship to the things of Middle-earth.

Not Just for Your Sole Benefit— The Land and Its Inhabitants

On the very last page of *The Hobbit*, Gandalf has one remaining piece of information. In the final words we hear Gandalf speak, the wizard explains to Bilbo: "You don't really suppose, do you, that all your adventures and escapes were managed by mere luck, just for your sole benefit? You are a very fine person, Mr. Baggins, and I am very fond of you; but you are only quite a little fellow in a wide world after all" (272).

Two concepts found here are central to Tolkien's vision of divine purpose. First, there has been a benevolent force at work *beyond mere luck* managing things—a topic discussed at length in the previous chapter. Second, this unseen hand is concerned with Bilbo's benefit and also with *something more than Bilbo's sole benefit*. Bilbo's story is a small part of a much larger story.

The unseen hand behind Bilbo's adventure has concern for him—a concern that has nothing to do with financial profit—and at the same time has concern for more than just his sole benefit. All along the two interests have been connected. Bilbo's adventure is a means. His own spiritual good is one of the ends, but only one. The hobbit's adventure is also a means for bringing good to the land around the Lonely Mountain and to its inhabitants.

Two maps are included in most editions of *The Hobbit*. In large letters right in the center of the map, which serves as a frontispiece, are words identifying the Desolation of Smaug. The arrival of the dragon has transformed the entire area shown—a formerly happy, fertile, and populous region—into a blasted, barren wasteland. The Lonely Mountain was originally given its name for being hundreds of miles from the nearest range of summits. Under Smaug it has become lonely in the additional sense that everything around it is now empty and lifeless.

At Bilbo's first meeting with Gandalf and the dwarves in chapter 1, Thorin tells how Smaug arrived, burning up the woods in a spout of flame. As the dwarves came out the front gate, the dragon was waiting and "none escaped that way" (23). Next, under cover of fog and steam from the river, Smaug picked off the warriors from Dale one by one. When Elrond looks at the map in chapter 3, Tolkien uses the opportunity to remind readers of the devastation Smaug has produced. We are told that it grieves Elrond to recall "the ruin of the town of Dale and its merry bells, and the burned banks of the bright River Running" (49). When Bilbo and the dwarves finally draw near to the Lonely Mountain, we find this stark description: "The land about them grew bleak and barren, though once as Thorin told them, it had been green and fair. There was little grass, and before long there was neither bush nor tree, and only broken and blackened stumps to speak of ones long vanished" (183).

It is only through Bilbo's discovery of the dragon's vulnerable spot that Bard is able to kill Smaug, and thus rid the land of the monster's tyranny so it may be renewed. In the book's final chapter, Balin reports that the valley has once again become tilled and bountiful and that the former desolation is now filled with "birds and blossoms in spring and fruit and feasting in autumn" (272). Not only has the land been healed of its wounds, but the adventure has also brought an end to the hostility between the region's inhabitants. Balin tells Bilbo there is now great friendship between elves, dwarves, and men.

In *The Fellowship of the Ring*, Tolkien provides one more window into this larger good that Bilbo's adventure has brought about. As Frodo and Gimli talk at the banquet at Rivendell, the dwarf tells of the continued goodwill between the dwarves and men, stating, "Nowhere are there any men so friendly to us as the Men of Dale" (222). After Gimli's account of how life, productivity, and prosperity have returned to the region, Frodo concludes, "How surprised Bilbo would have been to see all the changes in the Desolation of Smaug" (223).

Not Just for Your Sole Benefit— Thorin and Gollum

Two further benefits beyond Bilbo's sole good should be noted.

Several times in *The Hobbit,* we see evidence of Tolkien's training as a linguist and his sensitivity to the overtones a word or phrase may have. For example, in chapter 1 he has Gandalf point out the different meanings that Bilbo puts into the phrase "Good morning." In another example, as Bilbo witnesses the tumult of battle all around him, Tolkien has him exclaim, "Misery me!" (255), a somewhat odd phrase for Bilbo to use and one with deep religious overtones from the well-known Latin opening to Psalm 51, *Miserere mei, Deus* (Have mercy on me, God). In chapter 18, after reconciling with Thorin just moments before the dwarf's death, Bilbo states, "A mercy it is that I woke up when I did" (259). In fact, it has been a mercy, a real grace, not just for Bilbo, but also for Thorin, who has needed the example of Bilbo's goodness to prompt his return to the path of wisdom and who also needs the opportunity to take the final step in his redemption by apologizing to the hobbit. Here in Thorin's confession and restoration we see another way that Bilbo's adventure has not been just for his sole benefit.

In a similar manner, in *The Two Towers*, Tolkien will use the presence of Merry and Pippin to bring Boromir back to his right mind and to a similar deathbed statement of repentance. Aragorn tells the dying Boromir, "You have conquered. Few have gained such a victory" (404). These words speak of a great spiritual triumph, not a military one, and also serve as a fitting description of Thorin's final moral victory. Later, Faramir is given a mystical vision of Boromir's body in death and reports to Frodo that it is clear that his brother died well, "achieving some good thing" (654). After learning of Boromir's fate, Gandalf replies: "Galadriel told me that he was in peril. But he escaped in the end. I am glad. It was not in vain that the young hobbits came with us, if only for Boromir's sake. But that is not the only part they have to play" (485).

In *The Hobbit*, Thorin's soul, like Boromir's, is in peril. In the end, like Boromir, Thorin also escapes from the madness that overtook him and dies after achieving some good thing. Gandalf would say that Bilbo's role in Thorin's healing, though just one of the reasons he was selected, was not in vain.

If we can say that Bilbo plays a role in Thorin's rehabilitation, we can also say that there is the hope of potential benefit to Gollum because his path and Bilbo's cross.

In chapter 5 we are introduced to a small slimy creature named Gollum who lives alone deep below the Misty Mountains on an isolated island of rock that juts out of the subterranean lake. Though Tolkien's narrator claims not to know where he came from, we are offered a number of fragmentary glimpses of Gollum's former life. As he and Bilbo begin to talk, Gollum is reminded of a time before he lost all his friends and was driven away from his home, a time when he was less lonely, sneaky, and nasty. Gollum's five riddles and their solutions reveal the boundaries of his bleak existence: a *mountain* with roots no one sees; *wind* that mutters and bites; *darkness* that ends life and kills laughter; *fish* as cold as death; and *time* that devours, gnaws, grinds, slays, ruins, and beats. When we reach the climactic moment where Bilbo must decide whether to kill or spare Gollum, we share Bilbo's vision of Gollum's endless, unmarked days "without light or hope of betterment, hard stone, cold fish, sneaking and whispering" (80).

In *The Fellowship of the Ring*, Gandalf tells Frodo more of the sad story of the hobbit-like creature once called Smeagol, and expresses the wish that the evil side of Gollum might even yet be conquered or cured. With a sigh the wizard concludes, "Alas, there is little hope of that for him. Yet not no hope" (54). Out of hope for his cure, Gandalf has asked the Wood-elves holding Gollum to treat him with such kindness as they can. Given what we learn in other places, if Gandalf has hope for Gollum, we may assume that whoever sent Gandalf shares this hope. Gollum's cure is another of the many benefits that Bilbo's actions may have. Gandalf maintains that "the pity of Bilbo may rule the fate of many" (58), among them the fate of a very old and very wretched creature once called Smeagol.

Not Just for Your Sole Benefit— Many Paths and Errands

Fifty-nine years pass between Gandalf's final words in *The Hobbit* and Bilbo's next journey. As Bilbo sets off after his farewell party in *The Fellowship of the Ring*, he sings a walking song he has composed, and its lyrics reveal that he has understood what Gandalf meant by not "just for your sole benefit." The hobbit describes how the road goes on and on, leading from his door to a larger way where "many paths and errands meet" (35). The word *errands* here is a reminder of the divine purpose at work to benefit not just an individual but all of Middle-earth.

In "The Quest of Erebor," Thorin tells Gandalf that he is sure the wizard has other purposes besides helping the dwarves get back their treasure. Tolkien has Gandalf reply: "Great as your affairs may seem to you, they are only a small strand in the great web. I am concerned with many strands. . . . You and your quest are caught up in a much greater matter" (Anderson, 375). One of the many errands that Gandalf and those who sent him have is preventing Sauron from making use of Smaug in the war he is planning. Because Bilbo's path crosses Thorin's and Gollum's, many greater errands are accomplished to the benefit of many besides just Bilbo. This idea of a compassionate divine hand that works for our genuine benefit and simultaneously for the benefit of all is a concept well-known to Christians and one central to the Christian faith.

Of the many paths and errands that providentially meet in *The Hobbit*, Bilbo's encounter with Gollum is the most obvious. Less noticed, perhaps, is the path Bard has taken. In chapter 12, Smaug declares to Bilbo: "Girion Lord of Dale is dead, and I have eaten his people like a wolf among sheep, and where are his sons' sons that dare approach me?" (203). Two chapters later, we learn that one of Girion's sons' sons, Bard the Bowman, is alive and is in Lake-town—ready, 171 years later, to avenge his forebear's death. Readers are told: "He was a descendent in long line of Girion, Lord of Dale, whose wife and child had escaped down the Running River from the ruin long ago" (224).

Not only does Bard have a path graced with a providential hand that has brought him to his present position, so does the arrow he will use. "Black arrow!" Bard cries out as he prepares to shoot. "I have saved you to the last. You have never failed me and always I have recovered you. I had you from my father and he from of old. If ever you came from the forges of the true king under the Mountain, go now and speed well!" (224). In Bard's words "and always I have recovered you," readers may be reminded of the blade of Westernesse, which Merry uses to stab the Lord of the Nazgul in *The Return of the King*, a weapon that was also forged in the distant past. The short sword, which first comes to be in Merry's possession as Tom Bombadil's gift from the hoard in the Barrow-downs, is tossed aside by the orcs who capture Merry and Pippin, is recovered by Aragorn, is carried across Rohan, and is finally returned at Isengard. Though of less-noble lineage than Aragorn's famous sword, Anduril— Bard's arrow and Merry's blade follow a path that may seem like chance but is not. Like the three characters who wield them, each of these three weapons has an equally important errand to fulfill.

Bilbo's information about Smaug's weak spot, the presence of the old thrush, Bard, his Black Arrow, and even the path of the moon that night all seem to have been arranged to meet in this one critical moment. The dragon circles back, and we are told: "As he came the moon rose above the eastern shore and silvered his great wings" (224). The moonlight causes the gems covering his underbelly to glitter, except in one place, allowing the completion of the great errand that these many elements have combined to achieve. Smaug's demise in chapter 14 of *The Hobbit* is a critical juncture where many paths and errands meet for the benefit of many.

Thank Goodness

In chapter 1, when the dwarves doubt that Bilbo will be much help in their quest, Gandalf promises, "There is a lot more in him than you guess, and a deal more than he has any idea of himself" (19). Fifteen chapters later, when Bilbo brings the Arkenstone to Bard, Gandalf steps from the shadows to congratulate him on a deed well done. "There is always more about you than anyone expects!" the wizard again points out (245).

Although Bilbo possesses a rare abundance of virtues, Tolkien's deeper point is that there is unrecognized and undeveloped potential in every hobbit and, in our world by extension, unrecognized and undeveloped potential in every human. It has been Gandalf's business and the business of whoever sent him to help bring out this potential. Gandalf reminds us there is more about Bilbo than anyone expects. The same reminder could be said to be true for us as well.

When Bilbo finally recognizes the wizard in chapter 1, he exclaims: "Not the Gandalf who was responsible for so many quiet lads and lasses going off into the Blue for mad adventures? Anything from climbing trees to visiting elves— or sailing in ships, sailing to other shores! . . . I had no idea you were still in business" (7). Before his own mad adventure is fully finished, Bilbo himself will climb trees twice in *The Hobbit*, visit elves a number of times, and, in the final chapter of *The Return of the King*, sail to another shore. But in Bilbo's comment, Tolkien makes it clear that Gandalf's business is not confined only to him nor later to only Frodo, Sam, Merry, and Pippin, but extends to many other lads as well as lasses.

In *The Fellowship of the Ring* Tolkien returns to the idea of the great potential latent in every individual, even the most unlikely, telling readers: "There is a seed of courage hidden (often deeply, it is true) in the heart of the fattest and most timid hobbit, waiting for some final and desperate danger to make it grow" (137). Although Bilbo and Frodo may have been given a larger seed of courage than most, Tolkien makes it plain that this seed is present in all the Bagginses, Boffins, Tooks, Brandybucks, Grubbs, Chubbs, Burrowses, Hornblowers, Bolgers, and Bracegirdles—and in all of us.

While Tolkien saw the magnificent potential of each person, he also recognized the discrepancy between who we are and who we were made to be and the need for something that will bring out this greatness, a catalyst, like Gandalf sending Bilbo on an adventure. In *The Return of the King*, when Merry wants to raise the Shire, a spark is needed to ignite what has been dormant, or as Merry puts it, "They just want a match" (983).

In *The Two Towers* Tolkien offers this observation on the special purpose found in Middle-earth and the unseen purpose-giver. As Frodo and Sam pause for a brief rest high in the evil tower of Cirith Ungol, Sam reflects on adventures, confessing to Frodo: "I used to think that they were things the wonderful folk of the stories went out and looked for, because they wanted them, because they were exciting and life was a bit dull, a kind of sport, as you might say. But that's not the way of it. . . . Folk seem to have been just landed in them, usually—*their paths were laid that way*, as you put it" (696, emphasis added).

Many of Tolkien's contemporaries would have thought that the concept of a divine purpose laid out for a world and for each individual in that world was an idea that belonged only to an unenlightened, superstitious past. In a century that saw the image of what human beings are destined for become smaller and smaller, Tolkien celebrated their purpose and potential. For those desperately in need of a reminder of this divine purpose and enormous human potential, Tolkien can be a literal godsend. As Richard Purtill points out, Tolkien's world can serve as "a halfway house for those struggling out of the grayness of the modern view" (*Lord*, 154). "For Tolkien's view is a world of purpose," Purtill maintains, "a world where there is a real struggle between good and evil, a hope and a danger that go beyond the personal" (154).

On the last page of *The Hobbit*, where Gandalf tells Bilbo that there has been more than luck at work managing his adventures and escapes, that this unseen manager has been at work for Bilbo's benefit and something more, and that the hobbit is only a little fellow in a wide world, the hobbit's response is a hearty "Thank goodness!" (272). This phrase—which has its origins in "Thank God"—is Bilbo's final utterance in the book and is another of Tolkien's phrases that is rich with meaning. Thank goodness, it was not just mere luck but something more. Thank goodness that it was not just for my sole benefit. Thank goodness, I am only a little fellow in a larger story, for that is all I am up for.

Fifty-nine years after Gandalf and Balin's visit to Bag-End at the conclusion of *The Hobbit*, the Council of Elrond takes place at Rivendell. As depicted in *The Fellowship of the Ring*, the council finally arrives at the great question of who will take the ring to the fire of Mount Doom. Bilbo, who has been comfortably settled at Rivendell for many years and by this time is finally showing his age, stands and proclaims: "Say no more! It is plain enough what you are pointing at. Bilbo the silly hobbit started this affair, and Bilbo had better finish it, or himself. . . . When ought I to start?" (263).

Gandalf, who has been Bilbo's teacher and guide for many years, offers him one last piece of wisdom. "Of course, my dear Bilbo, if you had really started this affair, you might be expected to finish it," the wizard replies (263). Then Tolkien has Gandalf return to the point made on the final page of *The Hobbit*. "But you know well enough now that *starting* is too great a claim for any, and that only a small part is played in great deeds by any hero" (263).

So it is not only Bilbo who has played a small part but all of them. Everyone from Gandalf to Elrond to Aragorn to Frodo has a part to play, and in the grand scheme each of their roles is only a small part. But being a small player in a larger story actually enhances Bilbo's role instead of diminishing it. His adventure is only one thread in a great tapestry, but it is still a thread. Without his part, the tapestry would be incomplete. The fact that his story is not just his story but is part of a larger pattern in Middle-earth, where many paths and errands are intertwined, gives him and the decisions he makes a greater significance that extends well beyond himself.

If at the start of *The Hobbit* Gandalf promised that the adventure he was sending Bilbo on would be very good for him, years later at the Council of Elrond in *The Fellowship of the Ring*, Bilbo confesses to the wizard, "All your unpleasant advice has been good" (263). We can imagine Gandalf revisiting his claim from chapter 1 of *The Hobbit* and reminding Bilbo: "All my advice—pleasant or not—it has all been very good for you—and profitable too" (263).

You are only quite a little fellow in a wide world after all. Christians recognize that they, like Bilbo, have a part to play in the good of all the world, one that is a small part of a much larger design. Through his imaginary world of Middle-earth, Tolkien reminds us—and we need this reminder again and again—that our own world is also a place where many paths and errands meet and are intertwined, and not by chance nor without a special kind of good purpose.

Thank goodness.

Chapter 4

"I DON'T THINK I OUGHT TO": THE MORAL LANDSCAPE IN *THE HOBBIT*

A Moral Universe

In a letter to Peter Hastings, manager of Oxford's Newman Bookshop, Tolkien described his goal as a writer to be "the elucidation of truth" and "the encouragement of good morals in this real world" and claimed to do this through "the ancient device of exemplifying them in unfamiliar embodiments" (*Letters*, 194). Indeed, throughout his fiction, Tolkien acts as an usher, escorting us into Middle-earth, an imaginary pre-Christian world where he shines light on and clarifies the essential truths and moral laws of our own world. As Tolkien biographer Daniel Grotta-Kurska has pointed out, the good peoples of Middle-earth are "motivated and guided by a system of ethics that is Christian in everything but name" (138).

Tolkien's characters inhabit what writer Perry Bramlett calls "a moral universe" (188), in which they either initially or ultimately know what they should do, though they may sometimes hesitate to do it. In Tolkien's fiction, although the moral decisions characters must make are often complex and therefore difficult, there is always a choice that is right—not just right for that person or right for that situation, but right in a more universal sense. And if in Middle-earth there is always a choice that is right, there is also a choice that is wrong. In his portrait of absolute truth, objective right and wrong, and good and evil that is not relative, Tolkien presents a world that will feel familiar to Christian readers.

Tolkien's protagonists are what previous generations would have called *virtuous*, a word that has somewhat gone out of fashion in our time. Tolkien's readers, young and old, but perhaps particularly the young, find in his characters moving examples of faith, hope, love, perseverance, courage, and humility, examples that can serve as models to aspire to in their own lives. While Tolkien said he hoped his writing would lead to "the encouragement of good morals in this real world," readers today might express this concept a little differently.

They might say Tolkien's writing inspires them to do better and to be better, or perhaps that it inspires them to hold on and not give up. They might also say that Tolkien's stories remind them that the virtuous life is not dry, dull, or out of date—but high adventure.

Finding and Making the Right Choice

When Eomer meets Aragorn, Gimli, and Legolas on the plains of Rohan in *The Two Towers*, he must make a difficult decision of whether to obey the spirit or letter of the law about letting strangers wander freely. Eomer gives voice to a surprisingly modern-sounding uncertainty, complaining: "It is hard to be sure of anything among so many marvels. The world is all grown strange. . . . How shall a man judge what to do in such times?" (427). In the answer Tolkien gives Aragorn, we find the author's underlying position on right and wrong and our duty to distinguish between the two. "Good and ill have not changed since yesteryear," Aragorn replies. "Nor are they one thing among Elves and Dwarves and another among Men. It is a man's part to discern them as much in the Golden Wood as in his own home" (428).

C. S. Lewis has written that Aragorn's statement here about the existence of objective good and evil and our responsibility to distinguish between them forms "the basis of the whole Tolkienian world" ("Tolkien's," 87).

In the previous chapter of *The Two Towers*, when Aragorn expresses the need to choose their course rightly, Tolkien has Gimli respond, "Maybe there is no right choice" (406). Aragorn does not accept this implication of moral relativism, nor does Gandalf, nor does Tolkien. Three pages after Gimli's suggestion that there may be no right choices, Aragorn tells the dwarf and Legolas, "Let me think! And now may I make a right choice, and change the evil of this unhappy day!" (409). And in these words, we find Aragorn's conviction—and the author's—that in Middle-earth there is always a right choice to be made. A few chapters later, after Pippin steals a glance in the Palantir, Gandalf rejects the young hobbit's attempt to excuse his behavior by claiming he had no idea that what he was doing was wrong. The wizard states, "Oh, yes, you had. You knew you were behaving wrongly and foolishly" (584).

Three chapters after Aragorn's statement about the unchanging nature of good and evil, we find one of Tolkien's clearest examples of morals that are not based on the situation or on what might be most practical or advantageous. In *The Two Towers*, as Aragorn, Legolas, and Gimli search Fangorn for the missing hobbits, a mysterious old man approaches them, his face hidden beneath a hood and hat, a staff in his hands. Suddenly Gimli shouts to Legolas to use his bow. "It is Saruman," the dwarf declares. "Do not let him speak, or put a spell upon us! Shoot first!" (481). Even though they are now near Isengard, the home of Saruman, and even though they have been recently warned by Faramir that the traitorous wizard walks here and there appearing as an old man hooded and cloaked, Legolas does not fit an arrow to the string. Aragorn explains the moral principle restraining them. "Legolas is right," he states. "We may not shoot an old man so, at unawares and unchallenged, whatever fear or doubt be on us" (482).

As if to mirror the complex moral choices often found in the real world, Tolkien fills *The Hobbit* with difficult choices. In chapter 5 Bilbo must decide whether to kill Gollum or spare him, and in Bilbo's decision, Tolkien shows the type of careful thinking that must be done in complicated situations to discern what is right. Initially Bilbo decides it would be just to kill the vicious creature because it had meant to kill him. But then the hobbit comes up with four reasons why this would not be right: First, Bilbo is invisible, giving him an unfair advantage. Second, Bilbo has a sword and Gollum does not, another element that would make slaying him unfair. Third, Bilbo reasons that Gollum has not actually threatened to kill him, nor has he actually tried to yet. Finally, and most important, Bilbo sees Gollum with pity, as someone who is miserable, alone, and lost. After this careful and deliberate thinking, despite his fear and doubt, Bilbo knows what he must do. Strengthened and lifted by this resolve, he leaps over Gollum rather than killing him.

Bilbo faces similar difficult choices when he must decide whether or not to violate Thorin's trust and offer the Arkenstone to Bard, and then whether or not to return to the dwarves, where he will certainly face Thorin's wrath. In each of these difficult choices, the text suggests that there is a right choice. Richard Purtill writes that Bilbo finds himself in "a complex situation" (*Myth*, 66), one in which he must make "a lonely moral decision." In rejecting the offer of the Elvenking, who has promised that if the hobbit stays with them he will be honored and thrice welcome, Bilbo concludes, "I don't think I ought to leave my friends like this, after all we have gone through together" (244). Even in his choice of whether to keep the trolls' plunder or not there is a right decision to be discerned. In the end, Bilbo determines he must give it away since it was originally stolen.

Tolkien's pattern of carefully choosing amid doubts the path that is right can be found throughout his fiction. At the end of *The Fellowship of the Ring*, Frodo must choose whether or not to go to Mordor and whether or not to go alone. He first comments on the difficult choice he faces, telling Aragorn, "I know that haste is needed, yet I cannot choose. The burden is heavy" (387). After Frodo wrestles with his dilemma on Amon Hen, the Seat of Seeing, Tolkien makes it clear that in deciding to go to Mordor Frodo, he has found the right answer. We are told: "A great weariness was on him, but his will was firm and his heart lighter. He spoke aloud to himself. 'I will do now what I must'" (392).

Frodo initially thinks he should go alone, but Sam convinces his master that in this decision he is mistaken. Frodo agrees with Sam's correction using words that point to a greater plan, stating that it is plain that they were "meant" to go together (397).

In *The Two Towers*, Aragorn must decide whether to follow Frodo and Sam into Mordor or try to rescue Merry and Pippin. Then he, Gimli, and Legolas must decide whether to use precious time to bury Boromir or to set out while they still have a chance to catch the orcs and rescue the captives. Again we find words that point to a right answer. Legolas argues that no matter where they decide to go afterward or how much time it may cost, their first responsibility is to care for Boromir's body. He tells Aragorn and Gimli, "Let us do first what we must do" (405). This duty done, Aragorn then asks for time to think and carefully considers what they should do next. After standing for a time deep in thought, he concludes, "My heart speaks clearly at last: the fate of the Bearer is in my hands no longer" (409).

Here once again Tolkien suggests that after struggling between difficult choices, the right choice will ultimately be clear. In Aragorn's final words we can hear the implication that Frodo's fate, which Aragorn feels was put in his hands after Gandalf's death, has now been taken out of his hands—though Aragorn does not say by whom. At the same time, the fate of Merry and Pippin has now been given to him by this same unnamed authority and is now his responsibility. Later,

Gandalf confirms that Aragorn's choice was the right one, one that he should not regret or call vain, even though it did not accomplish what was intended.

In the final chapter of *The Two Towers,* aptly titled "The Choices of Master Samwise," Sam must discern whether or not he should take the ring and abandon Frodo, whom he believes to be dead. In one of Tolkien's most moving passages, we find Sam's struggle to decide what is right. Sam initially wishes Gandalf or one of the other leaders were present to help, and asks: "Why am I left all alone to make up my mind? I'm sure to go wrong. And it's not for me to go taking the Ring, putting myself forward" (715). But then, like Aragorn, Sam comes to see the responsibility that has been given to him by something or someone greater than himself. He concludes, "But you haven't put yourself forward; you've been put forward."

First believing his master to have been killed by Shelob, Sam makes the right decision and, in doing so, keeps the ring from falling into enemy hands. Pages later, after he learns that Frodo has only been stunned, Sam has a different right choice to make. Sam expresses his principle for his right action as long as Frodo is alive: "Never leave your master, never, never: that was my right rule" (724).

While finding the right answer is clearly needed in great decisions, the morality of right choices can also be seen in many of the small deeds in *The Hobbit* as well. In chapter 9, Bilbo makes sure to put the keys he has stolen back on the guard's belt with the hope it will save him some trouble when the elves learn of the escape. After turning over the Arkenstone to Bard in chapter 16, Bilbo is concerned that he get back in time to wake Bombur as he promised. He knows that if he is late, the wrath of Thorin will fall on Bombur for accepting the hobbit's offer to take his watch, and Bilbo does not want blame to extend to anyone but himself. In the final chapter, in return for the food and wine he took during the dwarves' imprisonment, Bilbo insists on giving the Elvenking a necklace of silver and pearls. Noting that it is the right thing to do, and implying that his conscience has been bothering him about his theft, Bilbo explains that "even a burglar" has feelings (263).

Just as in the real world, making the right choice in *The Hobbit* sometimes comes with a lightening of heart and sometimes with a painful sacrifice. Tolkien describes the moral dilemma Bilbo finds himself in at the start of chapter 6 as he wanders down the path after finally escaping from the goblin kingdom: "All the while a *very uncomfortable* thought was growing inside him. He wondered whether he ought not, now he had the magic ring, to go back into the horrible, horrible tunnels and look for his friends. He had just made up his mind that it was his duty, that he must turn back—and *very miserable* he felt about it—when he heard voices" (84, emphasis added).

Near the end of *The Fellowship of the Ring*, Galadriel describes the complex moral choices that make up the moral landscape of Middle-earth and the fact that despite the complexity, there is a right choice to be made, though in her case, it comes with a high cost. She tells Frodo that his mission spells doom for the elves either way: "If you fail, then we are laid bare to the enemy. Yet if you succeed, then our power is diminished, and Lothlorien will fade, and the tides of time will sweep it away" (356). With these two options, when Frodo asks her what is her wish, Galadriel responds, "That what should be shall be."

That what should be shall be. In these words we hear Tolkien's belief that there is a right choice, an outcome that should be. We also find an acceptance of that right choice despite the sacrifice. *That what should be shall be.* If we look at Bilbo's moral decisions in *The Hobbit*, this could be said to be his own guiding principle. *That what should be shall be.* In these words, we find Tolkien's version of "Thy kingdom come, thy will be done"—on Middle-earth as it is across the sea.

Motives, Even on the Right Side, Are Mixed

C. S. Lewis begins "The Dethronement of Power," his review of *The Lord of the Rings*, by stating, "There is one piece of false criticism which had better be answered: the complaint that the characters are all either black or white"

(11). He quotes Aragorn's statement, mentioned earlier, that "Good and ill have not changed . . . nor are they one thing among Elves and Dwarves and another among Men," and then Lewis comments that perhaps some readers who see (and dislike) Tolkien's clear demarcation between good and evil wrongly assume that Tolkien has created *characters* who can be classified as either totally good or totally bad. Lewis argues that this is not the case, rightly pointing out: "Motives, even on the right side, are mixed" (12).

Charles Huttar notes that while figures such as Gandalf and Sauron are at the extremes of Tolkien's "moral world" (135), even they are not purely good or purely evil. Sauron began as a good figure and has become evil through rebellion in a previous era. Gandalf, while on the opposite end of the moral spectrum, is also tempted by the ring and tries to avoid even touching it for fear he will not be able to resist its enticement. "In between these extremes," Huttar writes, "lie the vast majority of Tolkien's men, elves, dwarves, ents, wizards, and hobbits. They are never at any time automatically good or automatically evil. . . . Call the whole roll and the story is the same. They always possess the potential for good and evil, and every moment is one of decision" (135).

William Green also observes that Tolkien has sometimes been mistakenly accused of having characters that are "unrealistically polarized" at either end of the moral scale as being either totally good or totally evil (71). Taking a position similar to Huttar's, Green claims that while the goblins and

Elrond might be classified in this way, the other characters in *The Hobbit* cannot. Green maintains:

> Between the flanks of good and evil defined by Elrond on the one hand and goblins on the other . . . most of the other characters waver, choosing poorly or well. Beorn, though on the *side* of good, might have sent Bilbo's companions away to starve in Wilderland had he not been humored, and the Wood-elves, like the men of Esgaroth, are cruel or helpful according to their selfish purposes. (72)

Tolkien himself made it clear that the good peoples of Middle-earth are not all good—thus making their morality similar to our own. "I have not made the struggle wholly unequivocal," Tolkien claims (*Letters*, 262), and then he points to the stupidity and sloth that can be found in the hobbits, the pride that can taint the elves, the greed and grudge the dwarves can fall prey to, the men's folly and wickedness, and the power-lust and treachery that can affect the wizards. In another letter, he comments, "I have not made any of the people on the 'right' side . . . any better than men have been or are, or can be" (*Letters*, 244).

In *The Fellowship of the Ring*, a conflict emerges when Gimli—who, as a dwarf, must be blindfolded before entering Lothlorien—insists that Legolas also share his sentence. Haldir, following Aragorn's instructions, then blindfolds the entire company, stating: "Indeed in nothing is the power of the Dark Lord more clearly shown than in the estrangement that divides all those who still oppose him" (339). This divide among groups who share a common enemy, their petty jealousies, and their potential for conflict, can be seen in *The Hobbit* in virtually every encounter Bilbo and the dwarves have after they leave Rivendell.

After departing from the last homely house, the next home the group stays at is the rock shelf where the eagles have their nest. In chapter 6, the narrator explains that eagles are not "kindly" birds (95). They do not love goblins, but they do not make a special effort to oppose them and, in fact, often simply take no notice of them at all. Their offer of help is based on a past favor when Gandalf healed their leader of an arrow wound. Due to their habit of stealing sheep, the eagles are not on good terms with the men who live in the area. Because of this animosity, the eagles' offer of assistance is qualified. Their Lord tells Gandalf that while they are glad to cheat the goblins of their sport and glad to repay their debt to the wizard, they refuse to risk themselves for the dwarves by transporting them to the southward plains, which are inhabited by men.

After their stay with the eagles, the group next stays with Beorn. In chapter 7, Gandalf warns the others that they must be very polite when he introduces them and must be careful not to annoy Beorn, or heaven only knows what will happen. In addition, for fear of angering Beorn, who is one of the good moral characters in *The Hobbit*, Gandalf feels the necessity of introducing the dwarves two by two. When they reach the realm of the Wood-elves, the dwarves find even greater animosity as they are accused of attacking the party of merrymakers and are subsequently imprisoned, despite Thorin's truthful claim that the dwarves came only to beg because they were starving.

When they reach the town of the Lake-men in chapter 10, Bilbo and the dwarves initially receive a warm welcome, as the chapter title suggests. But this welcome is short-lived. By the chapter's end, readers are told that the Master is not sorry to see them go because they are expensive to keep and their arrival has created a long holiday during which business has come to a standstill. The next time they meet the Lake-men, it will be as armed enemies. In the Battle of Three Armies, which wages briefly before being miraculously transformed into the Battle of Five Armies, we find one of the clearest manifestations of the potential for moral failure that is always present in *The Hobbit*. At the heart of this distrust and animosity between the good peoples in *The Hobbit*—distrust and animosity that finally escalates into all-out conflict with bows twanging and arrows flying—is greed for material wealth.

The Power That Gold Has

Perhaps the most pervasive problem set by Tolkien within the moral landscape of *The Hobbit* is the excessive desire for wealth. A problem at the root of, if not *all* then *much* of the evil in Middle-earth, the desire affects men, elves, dwarves, hobbits, and goblins. It does not just affect *The Hobbit*'s dragon: Smaug serves as its embodiment. In chapter 3, as Elrond examines the dwarves' map, we are told that he does not altogether approve of the dwarves' love of gold. And neither does Tolkien.

In the unexpected party at Bag-End in chapter 1, Thorin declares that the dwarves have never forgotten the treasure they had to leave behind. Stroking the gold chain around his neck, he comments that even though they have a "good bit" beyond what was lost, they still intend to get back all that Smaug has stolen (23). A page earlier, the dwarf explained how dragons "guard their plunder as long as they live" and "never enjoy a brass ring of it" (22). These words will eventually come to describe Thorin's own brief time as the possessor of Smaug's hoard.

After the meal is finished and Bilbo's dishes put away, Thorin calls for some music. The dwarves sing of their resolve to obtain the jeweled swords, silver necklaces, crowns, goblets, and golden harps, which Smaug now guards. As they sing, Bilbo feels the dwarves' materialism— their love of "beautiful things made by hands"—awaken in him as well (15). This is not a good form of love, but a selfish love that is described as "fierce" and "jealous."

Knowing that most of his young readers would have relatively little personal interest in the typical objects found in a dragon's hoard, and so might think that his lesson about greed has nothing to do with them, Tolkien includes an unusual kind of treasure that Smaug also guards. Thorin tells Bilbo that during the height of their prosperity, the dwarves had the extra money and time to make beautiful things just for fun, a practice that led to creating marvelous and magical toys. Thorin concludes, "So my grandfather's halls became full of armor and jewels and carvings and cups, and the toy market of Dale was the wonder of the North" (22). In the very next sentence he states, "Undoubtedly that was what brought the dragon."

In *The Fellowship of the Ring*, Tolkien returns to the topic of dwarf-made toys. In his deliberate contrast between greed and generosity, he has Bilbo give very special toys to the hobbit children at his long-expected birthday party, the like of which had never before been seen in the Shire. The narrator reports that they are all beautiful and some are magical and had been special-ordered by Bilbo from the dwarf craftsmen at the Lonely Mountain and Dale.

When the dwarves are taken captive by the elves in chapter 8 of *The Hobbit*, we learn that money is at the root of their animosity. In the past, the elves had fought wars against the dwarves, whom they accused of stealing from them. The dwarves, of course, have a different account of the age-old grudge, claiming they were hired to shape the elves' gold and silver and then were never paid.

In a telling passage, Tolkien makes it clear that the dwarves are not the only race easily tempted by greed. The narrator explains: "If the elf-king had a weakness it was for treasure, especially for silver and white gems; and though his hoard was rich, he was ever eager for more, since he had not yet as great a treasure as other elf-lords of old" (152). When Thorin is questioned by the elves, he will not reveal the dwarves' real mission for fear of having to share some of Smaug's treasure, despite the fact that the elves have a legitimate claim to a portion of it. Later in chapter 17, the Elvenking tells Bard, "Long will I tarry, ere I begin this war for gold" (250), but he stops short of saying that he will never fight for a share of the treasure. He is simply not ready to fight quite yet.

Smaug, of course, is the epitome of greed—and each of the characters tempted by treasure risks becoming a smaller version of the dragon. In the final chapter, the Master of Lake-town is actually reported to have caught dragon-sickness, which leads to his death. After learning that Bilbo has taken just one cup from the vast hoard, the dragon goes into a frenzy. Smaug's fire belches forth, the hall is filled with smoke, and the mountain shakes. The narrator comments that Smaug's fury over the cup is the kind of rage that is seen only "when rich folk that have more than they can enjoy suddenly lose something that they have long had but have never before used or wanted" (196).

Promised a one-fourteenth share of the treasure, Bilbo falls under its spell on his initial visit to the dragon's lair. In chapter 12 Tolkien provides this description of Bilbo's first view of the hoard: "Bilbo had heard tell and sing of dragon-hoards before, but the splendor, the lust, the glory of such treasure had never yet come home to him. His heart was filled and pierced with enchantment and with the desire of dwarves; and he gazed motionless, almost forgetting the frightful guardian, at the gold beyond price and count" (194).

A chapter later, when the hobbit discovers the Arkenstone, a similar bewitchment overcomes him. Drawn by its enchantment, Bilbo's arm seems to have a will of its own as it suddenly reaches out for the gem. The jewel is so big, the hobbit's fingers will not fully close around it. Then we are told that Bilbo "lifted it, shut his eyes, and put it in his deepest pocket" (213). Although Bilbo later decides to give up the Arkenstone in an effort to avoid bloodshed, this is not his intention here. At this point in the story, he simply wants the glorious gem for himself. In taking it, Bilbo becomes not the honest burglar he later calls himself but a real one.

Thirty pages later Tolkien's narrator will make specific reference to "the power that gold has" (237). Here in chapter 13, the Arkenstone casts its power over Bilbo, causing him to excuse his theft of the jewel with a weak rationalization. "They did say I could pick and choose my own share," he thinks to himself (213). Despite the hobbit's attempt to justify his action, the narrator makes it clear that Bilbo knows his greed has got the better of him, stating: "All the same he had an uncomfortable feeling that the picking and choosing had not really been meant to include this marvelous gem, and that trouble would yet come of it" (213).

Immediately upon assuming possession of the dragon's hoard, Thorin becomes consumed by the desire to hold on to every bit of it—by force if need be. The desolation of Smaug threatens to become the desolation of Thorin. Partly convinced by Thorin's example of what greed can do and partly persuaded by his own conscience and good sense, Bilbo decides to give up the Arkenstone in the hope this will bring peace. Even so, as he hands the priceless gem over to Bard, it is not without a glance of deep desire, a dark craving that makes the hobbit shudder. Bilbo also gives up his claim to a one-fourteenth share of Smaug's hoard, mostly through a renunciation of excessive wealth but also partly due to his witnessing the epidemic of greed and violence that Smaug's treasure has brought on. Fearing that this greed and violence would accompany him all the way to Bag-End, he tells Bard, "How on earth should I have got all that treasure home without war and murder all along the way, I don't know" (261).

If Bilbo learns from Thorin's negative example, Thorin will also need Bilbo's positive example—as well as the arrival of the goblin army—to spur his repentance. As he nears death, we hear some of what Thorin has finally learned about true worth from the hobbit as he confesses, "If more of us valued food and cheer and song above hoarded gold, it would be a merrier world" (259). But even as the dwarf is on his deathbed, Tolkien points to the hold that gold still has over him as Thorin offers only this nuanced apology to Bilbo: "Since I leave now all gold and silver, and go where it is of little worth, I wish to part in friendship from you and I would take back my words and deed at the Gate" (258).

Since I leave now all gold and silver, and go where it is of little worth—in other words, if Thorin *could* take his material wealth with him to the afterlife, and if it *were* of worth there, perhaps he would not be so concerned about parting on good terms.

If the inordinate desire to lay up treasure on Middle-earth is one of Tolkien's central issues of *The Hobbit*, greed is also a central issue running throughout the New Testament, where again and again we find warnings against materialism. Believers are told that the love of money is the root of all evil (1 Timothy 6:10). Jesus tells his followers they cannot serve God and money (Matthew 6:24), and that it is easier for a camel to pass through the eye of a needle than for a rich man to enter heaven (Matthew 19:24). Christians are told to seek first the kingdom of God (Matthew 6:33), and that their hearts will be where their treasure is (Matthew 6:21).

Though his narrator often takes a light, grandfatherly tone, Tolkien intends to convey a serious message about the dangers of greed. At the end of *The Hobbit*, Tolkien gives us a final picture of one of the original thirteen dwarves, as Balin arrives at Bag-End with Gandalf for a visit. It is seven years since their adventure, and Balin has grown an impressive beard that is several inches longer than it was, and he now wears a magnificent jeweled belt, his version of the gold necklace Thorin wore in chapter 1. Like Bilbo, Balin has seen firsthand the destruction that greed can bring about, not only through Thorin's example and the barely averted war of dwarves, men, and elves, but also in the example of the old Master of Lake-town. Yet despite these cautionary tales, Balin, in the end, falls prey to its temptation himself.

During their discussion of dragon plunder in chapter 3, Elrond happens to comment, "I have heard that there are still forgotten treasures of old to be found in the deserted caverns of the mines of Moria" (49). The narrator points out that "Thorin pondered these words," but it is clear that after Thorin's death, Balin pondered them as well and never forgot them. At the Council of Elrond in *The Fellowship of the Ring*, Gloin tells the story of how Balin listened to words "whispered in secret," promising that "greater wealth and splendor would be found in a wider world" and how, against the wishes of King Dain, Balin resolved to lead a band of dwarves to Moria to seek after this wealth (234). As the dwarves had done in the past, Balin and his followers delve too deep and too greedily, waking an ancient evil that is their downfall.

Tolkien's Antidote to Greed: The Sacramental Ordinary

First, Bilbo gives away his share of the dragon's vast treasure in the form of the Arkenstone. Then, after he gets home, he gives away his portion of the trolls' plunder. In *The Fellowship of the Ring*, we find Bilbo once again embracing generosity over greed, and giving away another gift on par with the Arkenstone: his mithril coat. Frodo is staggered when he learns he has been walking about wearing "the price of the Shire" beneath his jacket (310). Frodo wonders whether Bilbo had known what an enormously expensive item he had given away, and readers are told, "He felt no doubt that Bilbo knew quite well. It was indeed a kingly gift." A chapter later, when Frodo's injury must be treated and the protective garment is revealed, Gimli comments, "Is this the coat that Gandalf spoke of? Then he undervalued it. But it was well given" (327).

Like the Arkenstone, the mithril shirt was very well given. Somehow, after only a brief struggle with it himself, Bilbo is able to avoid the greed that afflicts so many others— dwarves, elves, men, a dragon, and even his closest relatives, the Sackville-Bagginses. Tolkien suggests that Bilbo has found something of greater value than gold, something that might be labeled the "sacramental ordinary."

On the way home, in chapter 19, Bilbo once again stops at Rivendell, and in the song Tolkien has the elves sing, we find what the author puts forth as an alternative kind of treasure. The elves sing that the stars are brighter than gems, that the moon is whiter than silver, and that the fire on the hearth shines more than gold. They declare that after swords, thrones, crowns, strength in arms, and wealth are all rusted, withered, or gone, the growing grass, the fluttering leaves, the flowing water, and even the elves' singing itself will still remain.

Bilbo himself makes up a song with a similar theme as he comes over a rise and off in the distance sees his home for the first time since leaving a year before. He tells of the joy that is felt when eyes that have seen fire and sword now look on green meadows, trees, and hills they have long known.

Growing grass, fluttering leaves, flowing water, singing, green meadows, favorite trees, familiar hills—these ordinary things, Tolkien suggests, have something extraordinary about them. In the house of Tom Bombadil in *The Fellowship of the Ring*, the hobbits are invited to join in a song that praises and celebrates "sun, stars, moon and mist, rain and cloudy weather, light on the budding leaf, dew on the feather, wind on the open hill, bells on the heather, reeds by the shady pool, and lilies on the water" (120). This is the real treasure. These kinds of common, everyday things form the basis of Tolkien's sacramental ordinary.

As spring returns to the Shire in the final chapter *The Return of the King*, we find one of Tolkien's most definitive portraits of the sacramental ordinary and one of his most moving. There readers are told, "Not only was there wonderful sunshine and delicious rain, in due times and perfect measure, but there seemed something more: an air of richness and growth, and a gleam of a beauty beyond that of mortal summers that flicker and pass upon this Middle-earth"

(1000). This is what was driven out by the desolation of Smaug, the desolation of Mordor, and the desolation of Saruman. Several chapters earlier, Gandalf described the charge he had been given: to protect not the realms or kingdoms of Middle-earth, but its sacramental ordinary. The wizard told Denethor: "All worthy things that are in peril as the world now stands, those are my care. For my part, I shall not wholly fail of my task, though Gondor should perish, if anything passes through this night that can still grow fair and flower again in days to come" (742).

In the years following the events of *The Hobbit*, Bilbo will leave Bag-End once again and make his way to Rivendell where he meets Aragorn, the unassuming future king. After their own initial meeting with Strider at Bree in *The Fellowship of the Ring*, Frodo, Sam, and Pippin need convincing that he is who he says he is. Strider smilingly notes that his appearance is against him. Eventually Butterbur remembers the letter Gandalf left for Frodo, and in it the hobbits find a poem describing Aragorn and the unpretentious worth he embodies. The first line is "All that is gold does not glitter" (167). Several chapters later, at the Council of Elrond, when Boromir doubts Aragorn's claim to be a descendant of Elendil, Bilbo will stand and recite the poem again, whispering to Frodo afterward, "I made that up myself" (241).

Through his adventures in *The Hobbit*, Bilbo has learned two important truths: First, not all that glitters is gold. Even gold itself, while very glittery, is not the treasure it is said to be. Bilbo has also learned a parallel lesson: The real treasures of this world will not be all sparkling and dazzling on the surface. The real treasures of this world do not glitter, not in the superficial way that gold does.

Early in *The Two Towers*, one of the Riders of Rohan scoffingly asks: "Do we walk in legends or on the green earth in the daylight?" (424). "A man may do both," Aragorn answers. And in Aragorn's response we can hear Tolkien's own voice, suggesting that the ordinary world we live in every day is *as full of wonder as the material typically thought of as the stuff of legends*, and thus, is *equally deserving of our reverence*. As Tolkien has Aragorn explain: "The green earth, say you? That is a mighty matter of legend, though you tread it under the light of day!" (424).

A man may do both—and in Tolkien's fiction we do. We walk in legends and, just as important, we walk on the ordinary green earth in the daylight.

In commenting on G. K. Chesterton's impact on Tolkien, Joseph Pearce has written that there is considerable evidence of Chesterton's "indirect influence and . . . clearly discernible links of affinity between the two men" (164). Pearce argues that one of the most notable of these links is "the over-riding sense of wonder that permeates both men's work, and indeed both men's outlook and philosophy" (165). It is likely that Tolkien acquired some of his sense of the sacramental ordinary from his reading of Chesterton's classic work,

Orthodoxy, where Chesterton maintains, "Ordinary things are more valuable than extraordinary things; nay they are more extraordinary" (82).

Tolkien was also influenced and encouraged in the pursuit of the sacramental ordinary by his friend C. S. Lewis. Lewis's love of the commonplace began during his youth and was stimulated by his boyhood friend Arthur Greeves. In his autobiography, *Surprised by Joy*, Lewis writes about the love of the "homely" that Greeves helped to instill in him: "In his search for the homely he taught me to see other things as well. But for him I should never have known the beauty of the ordinary vegetables that we destine to the pot. 'Drills,' he used to say. 'Just ordinary drills of cabbages—what can be better?' And he was right" (157).

While on the one hand we could say that *The Hobbit* is made up of a wizard, dwarves, a hobbit, elves, a dragon, giant trolls, and fierce goblins, in his essay "On Fairy-Stories," Tolkien himself notes that the realm of Faerie also contains "many things besides elves and fays, and besides dwarfs, witches, trolls, giants, or dragons" (113). It also holds what we may

think of as more ordinary elements: "the seas, the sun, the moon, the sky, and the earth, and all the things that are in it: tree and bird, water and stone, wine and bread." Fairy-stories, Tolkien argues, deal mainly with "simple or fundamental things" from our own world that are "made more luminous" by their setting in an imaginary world (147). It was fairy-stories, he concludes, that helped him recover a proper wonder for simple things, a sense of the sacramental ordinary.

In a letter explaining what his stories were about, Tolkien claims that in his fiction he wanted to write about "ordinary life," which springs up "ever unquenched under the trample of world policies and events" (*Letters*, 160). In chapter 4 of *The Hobbit*, we are told that one of the characteristics of goblins, who embody the opposite of all that is right and good, is that they "hated everybody and everything" (59). Beginning with Bilbo's unexpected party in chapter 1 with its tea, seed-cakes, buttered scones, apple-tarts, mince-pies, cheese, eggs, cold, chicken, pickles, beer, coffee, and smoke rings, we find that *a reverence, celebration, and love of the everyday is an essential part of Tolkien's moral vision.*

In the end, Bilbo has learned to celebrate, love, and revere this sacramental ordinary. And if we have learned what Bilbo learns, so have we.

In addition to the song about green meadows, trees, and hills found in the last chapter of *The Hobbit*, if we turn to *The Fellowship of the Ring*, we find two more songs Bilbo has written in praise of these common things. After the hobbits reach Crickhollow and the end of the first stage of their journey, Pippin sings one of Bilbo's songs that honors the glories of an ordinary bath. It begins: "Sing hey! for the bath at close of day that washes the weary mud away! A loon is he that will not sing: O! Water Hot is a noble thing!" (99). At Rivendell, when Bilbo says farewell to Frodo, a deeply significant moment for both hobbits, he does so with a song that venerates commonplace wonders. Bilbo begins, "I sit beside the fire and think of all that I have seen" (271). He then goes on to list the many wonders he has experienced. Among these "wonders" Bilbo sings of are meadow flowers, butterflies, yellow leaves, the morning mist, and the wind in his hair.

Early in his essay "On Fairy-Stories," Tolkien raises the question, "What is the use of them?" (109). One use for fairy-stories, he argues, is *recovery,* and by this he means that these kind of stories help their readers to recover a proper sense of awe toward the commonplace. What we need, Tolkien writes, is to find a way to "clean our windows," so that the ordinary things of this world can be seen without the film of "triteness" (146). Tolkien claims that we have ceased to look at the common things of the world, and that fairy-stories help to move us from inattention to attention, and from indifference to appreciation.

Near the end of *The Hobbit,* Tolkien uses Thorin's deathbed, a place of great impact, to present one of the book's most important themes. In his final words, Thorin contrasts his values—the values that have led to nearly all of the strife and ruin in the story—with Bilbo's. While the dwarf has valued silver and gold, the hobbit has valued the common, everyday pleasures of life, in Thorin's words—"food and cheer and song"—Tolkien's sacramental ordinary (259). In Bilbo's values, Thorin finds wisdom and courage.

C. S. Lewis was well aware of the role the sacramental ordinary had in Tolkien's moral vision, and thus in his fiction, and in "The Dethronement of Power," Lewis argues that "the value of the myth is that it takes all the things we know and restores them to the rich significance which has been hidden by 'the veil of familiarity'" (14). Lewis maintains that we rediscover the commonplace—bread, horses, and even apples—when we encounter them in a myth. By "dipping" them in myth, we see these things more clearly (15).

In his essay "On Three Ways of Writing for Children," Lewis argues that fairy tales, the kind that both he and Tolkien wrote, give a "new dimension of depth" to the world their readers live in (38). "Far from dulling or emptying the actual world," Lewis writes, these stories restore to it something that has been eroded by the view, so dominant in the past century, that says it is nothing more than matter. We do not despise real woods because we have read of enchanted woods in fairy tales, Lewis concludes. "The reading makes all real woods a little enchanted."

In a poem titled "Mythopoeia," which he wrote for Lewis before his friend's conversion, Tolkien critiqued the view Lewis held at the time—called reductionism—which said the world and everything in it is reducible to matter and nothing more. "You look at trees and label them just so, / for trees are 'trees,' and growing is 'to grow,'" Tolkien begins (97). According to this view, a star is just a star, just "some matter in a ball." For Tolkien, trees and stars especially were far more than just trees and stars—both in our world and in Middle-earth.

The reading makes all real woods a little enchanted. The reading helps us look at our world with a new perspective, new wonder, and new appreciation. The reading helps us to see the sacramental ordinary that surrounds us.

In *The Return of the King*, as they rest together in the Houses of Healing, Pippin exclaims to Merry, "We Tooks and Brandybucks, we can't live long on the heights" (852). And neither can we. Tolkien closes both his great works with a final celebration of the sacramental ordinary. After a story involving trolls, spiders, elves, goblins, wargs, a shape-shifter, and a dragon, Tolkien ends *The Hobbit* with Bilbo, Gandalf, and Balin back at Bag-End, comfortably settled in chairs around a cozy autumn fire, with Bilbo passing Gandalf the tobacco jar. After more than a thousand pages of epic adventure, Tolkien ends *The Lord of the Rings* with Sam's return to Hobbiton. The narrator offers this description on the last page of *The Return of the King*:

But Sam turned to Bywater, and so came back up the Hill, as day was ending once more. And he went on, and there was yellow light, and fire within; and the evening meal was ready, and he was expected. And Rosie drew him in, and set him in his chair, and put little Elanor upon his lap.

He drew in a deep breath. "Well, I'm back," he said. (1008)

Tolkien intends for his readers to see that these everyday, ordinary elements of Middle-earth are not the icing on the cake, but the very cake itself. They are not something that is thrown in along with the other more spectacular rewards of victory. They are the main prize.

In a letter written in 1958, Tolkien makes his now-famous statement: "I am in fact a Hobbit (in all but size)" (*Letters*, 288). The author then goes on to list the many simple enjoyments that both he and hobbits love, among them gardens, trees, unmechanized farmlands, good plain food, ornamental waistcoats, mushrooms, and a simple sense of humor. Through his fiction, Tolkien helps us learn to love these things as well, and in these ordinary things to see something we may not be seeing, something extraordinary.

In a touching scene near the middle of *The Fellowship of the Ring*, Frodo is reunited with Bilbo in Rivendell's Hall of Fire. Soon, however, the two hobbits retire to Bilbo's room, for they have much to talk about. Once there, we are told, they look out on the night sky and the wood-covered hillsides, and they do not speak of small news of the Shire, nor of the great perils that surround them, but of the fair things they have seen together. Among them, we are told, are the stars, the trees, and the "gentle fall of the bright year in the woods" (232).

Tolkien's sacramental ordinary.

Not by Might, Not by Power

Of course, the most crucial ordinary elements in Tolkien's fiction—at least as the world typically defines *ordinary*—are the hobbits themselves. In the opening chapter of *The Hobbit*, Gloin sizes up Bilbo's limitations and reports: "As soon as I clapped eyes on the little fellow bobbing and puffing on the mat, I had doubts. He looks more like a grocer than a burglar!" (18). At the end of *The Hobbit*, Tolkien has Gandalf remind Bilbo that he is only "quite a little fellow" in a wide world (272).

In the section appropriately titled "Concerning Hobbits" from the prologue of *The Fellowship of the Ring*, Tolkien writes that hobbits are an unobtrusive people who "love peace and quiet and good tilled earth" (1), a race of little people who seem "of very little importance" (2). "But," Tolkien concludes, "in the days of Bilbo, and of Frodo his heir, they suddenly became, by no wish of their own, both important and renowned, and troubled the counsels of the Wise and the Great." Later, when Frodo asks why he has been chosen, Gandalf assures him that it was "not for power or wisdom, at any rate" (60). At Rivendell, Elrond points out that the road the company must tread will be hard. Then Tolkien has Elrond explain: "And neither strength nor wisdom will carry us far upon it. This quest may be attempted by the weak with as much hope as the strong" (262).

Christian readers may be reminded of similar words used in 1 Corinthians 1:26-27 to describe the way God chooses to work through the lowly: "For ye see your calling, brethren, how that not many wise men after the flesh, not many mighty, not many noble, are called: But God hath chosen the foolish things of the world to confound the wise; and God hath chosen the weak things of the world to confound the things which are mighty."

In book 12 of *Paradise Lost*, Milton's Adam comes to a similar vision of the way the humble are used by God to confound the mighty—"with good still overcoming evil, by small accomplishing great things, by things deemed weak subverting worldly strong, and worldly wise by simply meek" (246).

In the opening chapter of *The Hobbit*, we are told that the hobbits have little or no magic about them besides the "ordinary everyday sort," which allows them to disappear quietly when they want to (4). Tolkien makes it clear that Bilbo does not have any more special ability than anyone who is reading about his adventure. You *are only quite a little fellow in a wide world after all.* And so it is with each of us.

In his essay titled "Tolkien's *The Lord of the Rings*," C. S. Lewis points out the paradox between the quiet, unobtrusive hobbits and the great destiny to which some of them are called. As he notes, any hobbit "may find himself forced out of the Shire and caught up into that high conflict" (85). But stranger still, Lewis concludes, "that conflict between the strongest things may come to depend on him, who is almost the weakest."

After the climactic battle that ended the Second Age of Middle-earth, long before the time when *The Hobbit* and *The Lord of the Rings* takes place, two mighty elf-lords and a powerful king of men stood beside Mount Doom with Sauron's ring, the one ring, which, in the final conflict, had just been cut from his hand. Though Elrond and Cirdan counseled Isildur to cast the ring into the fires it was forged in, they failed. Isildur claimed the ring as a wergild for his father's death, and because the ring was not destroyed, Sauron was able to return to power. Now in the Third Age, the Authority behind the events in Middle-earth again seeks to have Sauron and the ring forever destroyed. But this time, the unnamed Authority will use three ring-bearers who are neither mighty elf-lords nor powerful kings. Bilbo, Frodo, and Sam are peace-loving hobbits whose only special qualities are their profound love for their homeland, their deep sense of duty, and their amazing perseverance. And this time they will succeed, but not by might, nor by power.

Colin Duriez notes that in Tolkien's fiction, Middle-earth is saved by "ordinary people, not by the mighty, powerful, and wise," but by "unheroic, humble figures like Bilbo, Frodo, Sam, and Merry" (181). In Tolkien's choice of humble saviors for Middle-earth, some readers may think of an uneducated carpenter's son born in a stable and his ragtag followers, who at the start were merely fishers of fish.

"Why did Tolkien have a rather uninteresting character, rather than Bilbo, kill Smaug?" asks Dorothy Matthews (38). "Why is Bilbo, the previous center of interest, knocked unconscious so that he is useless during the last Battle of Five Armies? Isn't it a fault in artistic structure to allow the protagonist to fade from the picture during episodes when the normal expectation 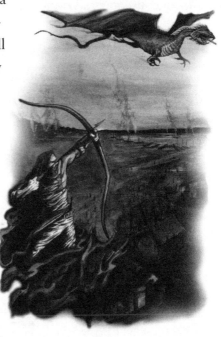 would be to have him demonstrate even more impressive heroism?" The answer is that Tolkien wanted to tell a story where the weak and lowly are used to confound the mighty and strong, and in doing so to share this key aspect with the gospel story.

Tolkien was not the only twentieth century writer to feature a common, ordinary character as a protagonist. In "The Love Song of J. Alfred Prufrock," T. S. Eliot also puts an average, unassuming, middle-aged character center stage. Although both Bilbo and Prufrock are humble figures, and both like their tea, tea cakes, and marmalade, the difference ends there. Prufrock has agonizing internal debates about such inconsequential topics as whether he should dare eat a peach or comb his hair over his bald spot. Bilbo begins with worries about chipped plates and pocket handkerchiefs, but ends up making decisions that will affect the fate of men, dwarves, and elves. The difference between the two is the potential each author sees in these ordinary characters. While Prufrock remains condemned to live in a wasteland, Bilbo plays a key role in restoring one.

Tolkien once noted in a letter that there were certain themes that especially moved him. High among them was the "ennoblement of the ignoble" (*Letters*, 220). While Bilbo, Frodo, Merry, Pippin, and Sam start out as ordinary hobbits, their nobility is manifest in the end—and along with it, Tolkien's suggestion that there is something noble about ordinary humans as well. Eliot has Prufrock declare that he is not Prince Hamlet and was never meant to be. In his grim world of yellow smog and indecision, Eliot suggests there is nothing particularly noble about humanity. In Eliot's world, the ignoble remain ignoble.

A similar contrast can be made between Bilbo and another humble, modern hero—Arthur Miller's Willy Loman. Again we find radically different positions regarding the inherent worth of the individual. In *The Hobbit*, Thorin and readers alike come to have a "very high opinion" of Mr. Baggins and come to see him as remarkable (159). In *Death of a Salesman*, Willy proves to be not only *not* vital in New England, as he claims, but a dime-a-dozen man who is worth more dead than alive.

In the Sermon on the Mount, Jesus announced, "Blessed are the meek: for they shall inherit the earth" (Matthew 5:5). In Middle-earth we might say, "Blessed are the Halflings," or using the line from Boromir's dream in *The Fellowship of the Ring*, "The Halfling forth shall stand" (240). In Tolkien's fiction, the meek, under the guidance of an unseen hand, help save and restore the earth. The world—both ours and Tolkien's—does not view the meek with much regard. In *The Hobbit*, Gloin sees Bilbo as a grocer. In *The Two Towers*, one of Eomer's men scoffs that Halflings are only a "little people in old songs and children's tales" (424). In *The Return of the King*, Denethor declares it madness to send the ring to Mount Doom in the hands of a "witless halfling" (795).

"Not by might, nor by power, but by my spirit," says the Lord in Zechariah 4:6. *Not by might, nor by power*—here we find Tolkien's principle for the way things are accomplished in Middle-earth and in our own world as well.

In the moral landscape of *The Hobbit*, readers find an ethical setting that is strangely familiar—a world where free will, personal responsibility, and the need to discern and make right choices are critical; a world where greed is pervasive and must be countered by embracing a very different kind of value.

Tolkien intends this world to be not just strangely familiar, but to be a world that feels very much like home.

RESPONSE AND LEGACY

A Terrifying and Bitter Adventure?

In October 1937, about a month before its publication, Tolkien received comments about *The Hobbit* from author Richard Hughes, who had been sent an advance copy. Hughes reported that *The Hobbit* was one of the best stories for children he had read in a long time and, in fact, he had only one concern. This snag, as he called it, was the possibility that parents might think some parts of it would be "too terrifying for bedside reading" (*Letters*, 23).

Tolkien responded to Hughes's concern by maintaining that having parts that were terrifying was both necessary and unavoidable because Middle-earth was intended to mirror our own world. He explained, "The presence (even if only on the borders) of the terrible is, I believe, what gives this imagined world its verisimilitude. A safe fairy-land is untrue to all worlds" (*Letters*, 24).

The presence of the terrible makes Middle-earth seem real and true. A safe fairyland would seem untrue. Perhaps here Tolkien was thinking beyond *The Hobbit* to some of the highly sanitized versions of fairy tales that were at the time beginning to replace their darker, and thus more real, original versions on page and screen. Shortly after the British release of *The Hobbit*, Tolkien received a request that some additional illustrations for the American edition of the book be created by American artists. Tolkien responded that he was willing to approve this as long as it was possible to veto "anything from or influenced by the Disney studios," for whose works Tolkien claimed he had a "heartfelt loathing" (*Letters*, 17).

For a story written for the young and the young at heart, *The Hobbit* contains a fair measure of violence and bloodshed. Although some scenes, such as the encounter with the trolls, are cast in a humorous light, Tolkien's story is, at times, genuinely scary. In chapter 4, Bilbo and the dwarves are snatched in the night and hauled away through a crack in the back of the cave where they had sought shelter. In the daring rescue, Bilbo and readers as well watch as Gandalf's sword goes right through the Great Goblin. Young readers will certainly find Bilbo's encounter with the slimy and hissing Gollum creature to be frightening, with his horrible swallowing noise and big pale eyes.

Wargs, more goblins, spiders, and a terrible dragon add to the fearsome elements Bilbo and readers meet in the story. We find this chilling description of Bilbo's encounter with the great spider: "He could feel its hairy legs as it struggled to wind its abominable threads round and round him. . . . Bilbo came at it . . . and struck it with his sword right in the eyes. Then it went mad  and leaped and danced and flung out its legs in horrible jerks, until he killed it with another stroke; and then he fell down and remembered nothing more for a long while" (141).

Partway through *The Lion, the Witch and the Wardrobe*, C. S. Lewis has his narrator break in to say that he is not going to describe the "Cruels and Hags and Incubuses, Wraiths, Horrors, Efreets, Sprites, Orknies, Wooses, and Ettings" that are part of the White Witch's troops, claiming: "If I did the grown-ups would probably not let you read this book" (151). Lewis is half-joking but half-serious. He was aware of critics who thought stories for children should never be frightening. While he was sympathetic to their concerns, he did not agree with their arguments.

In his essay "On Three Ways of Writing for Children," Lewis expresses the need for courageous knights and daring bravery in stories for young people as a counter to the cruel enemies that children will meet in their own lives. "Let them at least have heard of brave knights and heroic courage," Lewis concludes. "Let there be wicked kings and beheadings, battles and dungeons, giants and dragons, and let villains be soundly killed at the end of the book" (39–40).

G. K. Chesterton, a great influence on both Tolkien and Lewis, makes a similar point in an essay titled "The Red Angel." There Chesterton explains:

> A lady has written me an earnest letter saying . . . it is cruel to tell children fairytales, because it frightens them. . . . This kind of talk is based on that complete forgetting of what a child is like. If you keep bogies and goblins away from children they would make them up for themselves. . . . Exactly what the fairytale does is this: it accustoms them . . . to the idea that these limitless terrors have a limit, that these shapeless enemies have enemies, that these strong enemies of man have enemies in the knights of God, that there is something in the universe more mystical than darkness, and stronger than fear. (128–30)

In words similar to Tolkien's comments about a safe fairyland being untrue, Chesterton maintains: "Fairytales do not give the child the idea of the evil or the ugly; that is in the child already, because it is in the world already. Fairytales do not give the child his first idea of bogey. What fairytales give the child is his first clear idea of the possible defeat of bogey" (130).

Chesterton concludes his discussion this way: "At the four corners of a child's bed stand Perseus and Roland, Sigurd and St. George. If you withdraw the guard of heroes you are not making him rational; you are only leaving him to fight the devils alone" (132). If Chesterton were writing about today's children, boys and girls who are likely to have never heard of Perseus or Roland, he might have said at the four corners of a child's bed stand Gandalf, Bilbo, Bard, and Beorn.

If at times *The Hobbit* is genuinely frightening, it is also at times genuinely grim and sorrowful. In chapter 17 Bilbo wakes on the battlefield, his body shaking with shock and cold. His head, where it was battered with a stone, is burning with fire. The weary hobbit looks around and concludes that even in victory, warfare is a "very gloomy business" (257). When the soldier sent to look for him asks if he is hurt, Bilbo reports that he received a horrid knock on the head, his legs are as weak as straws, and he feels sick.

The hobbit is carried to a tent where Thorin, who is "wounded with many wounds," waits only to make amends before dying (258). Bilbo says his final farewell as he kneels in sorrow by the bedside. "This is a bitter adventure, if it must end so," he concludes, adding that "not a mountain of gold can amend it." After Thorin's final words, Bilbo turns away and sits off by himself wrapped in a blanket, where he weeps until his eyes are red and his voice is hoarse.

Why include scenes of such bitter sadness in a book for young people? To paraphrase Tolkien, we might say that a sorrowless fairyland would seem untrue. We might say the presence of sadness is needed to give Tolkien's imagined world its verisimilitude. If, to avoid this sadness, at the last moment Gandalf had raised his staff and—with flash of light and a great poof—restored Thorin to life by some unexplained magical power Tolkien had invented at the last minute, it would have seemed false.

In his famous essay "On Fairy-Stories," Tolkien offers another argument for the inclusion of darker elements that other writers might have left out. There Tolkien maintains, "Children are meant to grow up, and not to become Peter Pans. Not to lose innocence and wonder; but to proceed on the appointed journey" (137). He concludes that depicting peril, sorrow, and death in a fairy-story can "bestow dignity and even sometimes wisdom" on youth who are in need of these virtues.

Several equally sorrowful counterparts to Bilbo's farewell to Thorin can be found in *The Return of the King*. As Theoden lies dying after the Battle of the Pelennor Fields, his final words are to Merry, who, the narrator reports, is so anguished that for a time he weeps so hard he cannot speak. As Sam says his last farewell to Frodo, Tolkien reports that he is "sorrowful at heart" and finds their parting bitter (1007). And as Aragorn goes to his final rest, we are told that Arwen is "overborne by her grief" (1037). In each of these cases, we may wonder, as Merry does, Where is Gandalf? Could he not have done something?

But in each of these sorrowful instances, Tolkien does not end in sadness. Bilbo's final words to Thorin in *The Hobbit* are that his has been a bitter adventure *if it must end so*, but it does not end so. Tolkien goes on to end the story with reconciliation, restoration, and return.

In *The Return of the King*, we find a similar pattern. Though his body is battered and broken, as he goes to be with his ancestors, Theoden tells Merry, "I shall not now be ashamed" (824). The King of Rohan ends his life not in darkness and despair, but with a "golden sunset." When Eomer arrives, he gives voice to Tolkien's formula for sorrow, telling those around the fallen king, "Mourn not overmuch!" (825).

Eomer does not forbid mourning or suggest it is wrong to mourn, but says not to mourn *overmuch*. And in these words Tolkien reminds us that, to paraphrase Chesterton, there is something in the universe stronger than sorrow, something that puts a limit to sorrow.

In Aragorn's parting words to Arwen, also found in *The Return of the King*, we find perhaps the clearest expression of Tolkien's position on grief, and this position rings true both in our world and in Middle-earth. Aragorn begins by stating, "In sorrow we must go" (1038), and other authors would have stopped here. Other authors would not have suggested there is something beyond sorrow, because they did not believe there was. Tolkien did. "In sorrow we must go, but not in despair," he has Aragorn tell Arwen. "Behold! we are not bound for ever to the circles of the world, and beyond them is more than memory" (1038).

In the poem Bilbo writes for Aragorn in *The Fellowship of the Ring*, we find another expression of Tolkien's formula for hurt and healing. In one of the lines, Bilbo states, "Deep roots are not reached by the frost" (241). Yes, there will be killing frosts, but they will not destroy everything, not by a long shot. Yes, a fire may burn out and seem to be nothing but ashes, but in another line from Bilbo's poem Tolkien asserts, "From the ashes a fire shall be woken." To paraphrase Chesterton again, we might say that fairy tales do not give the child his or her first idea of sorrow. What fairy tales give the child is the idea of comfort for sorrow and the possibility of healing and hope.

Since the very last sentence of *The Hobbit* tells of Bilbo's laughter as he hands Gandalf the tobacco jar, we could say that Tolkien ends the story with joy and amusement. Back in chapter 1, when Gandalf tells Bilbo he will send him on an adventure, he comments, "Very amusing for me" (7). This scene from the opening chapter ends with the wizard laughing long but quietly outside the door to Bag-End. Surely much of Gandalf's amusement will come from seeing Bilbo having to face a world without his pocket handkerchiefs, tea cakes, and fine plates. But perhaps Tolkien is also having Gandalf look beyond the adventure to the happiness that he can see at the very end. This same happiness and ultimately positive view of the adventure are reflected in Bilbo's choice of subtitle for his memoirs. In the book's final scene, we find Mr. Baggins in his study, hard at work on *There and Back Again*, and the subtitle he has selected for his book is *A Hobbit's Holiday*.

If You Like It, You Do

In a letter written to his publisher, Stanley Unwin, on October 15, 1937, three weeks after the British release of *The Hobbit*, Tolkien offers the following report on the local reaction to his book:

> I think "Oxford" interest is mildly aroused. I am constantly asked how my hobbit is. The attitude is (as I foresaw) not

unmixed with surprise and a little pity. My own college is I think good for about six copies, if only in order to find material for teasing me. Appearance [of a review] in *The Times* convinced one or two of my more sedate colleagues that they could admit knowledge of my "fantasy" (i.e. indiscretion) without loss of academic dignity. The professor of Byzantine Greek bought a copy, "because first editions of *Alice* are now very valuable." (*Letters*, 24–25)

Unwin wrote back, telling Tolkien: "It is seldom that a children's writer gets firmly established with one book, but that you will do so very rapidly I have not the slightest doubt. . . . You are one of those rare people with genius, and, unlike some publishers, it is a word I have not used half a dozen times in thirty years of publishing" (*Letters*, 25).

We could say that in the middle of a comfortable and settled life, Tolkien found himself writing works that were altogether unexpected of an Oxford professor. Like Bilbo, in the end Professor Tolkien lost more than spoons—he lost the respect of some of his neighbors as well as a fair amount of his academic reputation. But like Bilbo, Tolkien did not really mind, for he gained something far greater.

There is something about Tolkien's fiction that does not seem to allow for a moderate opinion. Readers tend to either really like it or really dislike it, and it has been this way from the start. In response to the negative criticism he received, Tolkien commented, "Some critics seem determined to represent me as a simple-minded adolescent" (*Letters*, 244).

Summarizing the highly polarized reaction, especially to *The Lord of the Rings*, and the great gulf separating the two responses to his work, Tolkien wrote this verse:

The Lord of the Rings
is one of those things:
if you like you do:
if you don't, then you boo! (Carpenter, 226)

And much the same could be said for *The Hobbit*. In the debate over Tolkien's stories of Middle-earth, there seems to be very little middle ground.

In an interview, Tom Shippey was asked why in general Tolkien has been so popular with readers but so unpopular with critics. Shippey comments that while one reason Tolkien is so well-liked by readers is simply his skill as a writer, there is a deeper reason behind the popularity of his works. Shippey observes that in his fiction, Tolkien addresses "questions that have deeply preoccupied ordinary people, but that have not been answered by the official (or self-elected) speakers of our culture—writers, politicians, philosophers" ("Interview," 18). In Tolkien's works critics see "a challenge to the dominant literary orthodoxy of the past century, which has been ironic and self-doubting," Shippey continues. Calling it "shallow and unthinking," they reject Tolkien's "essentially positive and optimistic view of humanity" (18).

Many who are quick to label Tolkien's fiction as light-weight because it is fantasy somehow ignore the fact that many highly respected works of the past and present are also fantasy. Professional arbiters of literary taste who have no problem with the fantasy elements in *The Odyssey*, *The Tempest*, or *1984* often reject these same elements in *The Hobbit*. Serious literary critics fondly embrace *The Lord of the Flies*, where chaos and murder overcome reason and goodness, but dismiss *The Lord of the Rings*, where good overcomes evil. William Golding was awarded the Nobel Prize for literature. J. R. R. Tolkien has been and continues to be largely ignored by the literary establishment, and when not ignored, is typically derided.

Tolkien's Comments "On Fairy-Stories"

On a cold spring day in 1939—less than a year and a half after *The Hobbit* was published—Tolkien boarded a train bound for the windswept eastern coast of Scotland and the campus of the University of St. Andrews. There, on March 8, he presented an invited lecture he titled "On Fairy-Stories." Tolkien's lengthy and sometimes convoluted presentation, part of the prestigious Andrew Lang Lectures, would go on to become the most famous address in the series. With *The Hobbit* still firmly in his mind, this lecture, now published in written form and quite well-known among Tolkien fans, provides a unique window into the author's intentions in writing his own fairy-stories.

One point Tolkien makes in "On Fairy-Stories" is that it is only in recent literary history that this type of story has been labeled for children only and consequently "relegated to the nursery" (130). Any fairy-story that is worth reading at all, he claims, will be worthy to be read by adults as well. Adults, of course, will get more out of the same story read in their childhood—an observation with which readers of *The Hobbit* and *The Lord of the Rings* would heartily agree. Books, like clothes, should allow for growth, Tolkien argues.

In Tolkien's statements, we can hear echoes of C. S. Lewis's assertion, mentioned earlier, that *The Hobbit* is a children's book "only in the sense that the first of many readings can be undertaken in the nursery" ("Hobbit," 82). It will be only years later, Lewis states—when we go back and reread the story of Bilbo's adventure for "a tenth or a twentieth" time—that we will begin to fully see the great skill and deep reflection that went into its creation.

In a letter written in 1955, sixteen years after his seminal lecture, Tolkien repeated his point that fairy tales are not just for children and argued that there exists a deep human need for this kind of story. Tolkien comments, "It remains an unfailing delight to me to find my own belief justified: that the 'fairy-story' is really an adult genre, and one for which a starving audience exists" (*Letters*, 209).

In "On Fairy-Stories," we also find Tolkien's theory about the creative work of an author. Tolkien saw God as the only primary creator. Being created in God's image, man is also a creator of sorts. But unlike God, man does not create from nothing. He is like a carpenter who has been given the wood to build with, and hence, Tolkien suggests, should be thought of as a *sub-creator*. God created the universe, which Tolkien calls the Primary World. Tolkien's world of Middle-earth, found in *The Hobbit* and *The Lord of the Rings*, he classifies as a Secondary World.

In the next part of his lecture, Tolkien points to three ways that fairy tales function for their readers. The first thing these stories provide is *recovery*. By recovery, Tolkien means regaining a clear view, something we have lost. Fairy-stories help us to see the things of our world as we were meant to see them, with wonder instead of triteness—to see them afresh, not hidden behind dull familiarity. Through fairy-stories we get back a sense of the sacramental quality in the common, everyday things of creation that surround us.

Paul Pfotenhauer has pointed out that Tolkien has the faculty of "broadening and sharpening" his readers' vision, so that once again they begin "to look for and recognize the evidence of things unseen as well as things seen" (13). In Tolkien's world, he concludes, "The supernatural ceases to be mere superstition and is again seen as very real"—opening readers to the possibility of the existence of something greater than ourselves, something that is "the guiding factor in the events of our life and world" as well.

In *Surprised by Joy*, C. S. Lewis notes, "A young man who wishes to remain a sound atheist cannot be too careful of his reading" (191). While Lewis is commenting here on the role that the works of G. K. Chesterton and George MacDonald played in his conversion, his caution could also be extended to the effect Tolkien's works can have in changing how we see the world.

A second benefit that Tolkien claims fairy-stories provide is *escape*—though not the negative kind of escape he is often accused of providing. While some critics charge Tolkien with taking his readers away from reality, he would argue the exact opposite: that stories like the kind he wrote point readers toward reality. In "On Fairy-Stories," Tolkien goes on to state that much of the "serious" literature of today resembles "play under a glass roof" at a municipal swimming pool (150). Fairy tales, he claims, peel back this roof and show readers the sea and the heavens.

Do readers, young and old, run to *The Hobbit* or *The Lord of the Rings* simply to escape the distress, disappointment, and dullness of our own world? In Tolkien's works, we do not find an escape from pain, discomfort, drudgery, doubt, or sorrow, for there is plenty of all these things in Middle-earth. Nor are we offered an escape from evil. In fact, Tolkien may even provide his readers with a heightened sense of the existence of evil and of the power it has. When

Aragorn speaks about the Black Riders in *The Fellowship of the Ring*, Tolkien has him warn the hobbits, "You fear them, but you do not fear them enough" (162). Tolkien makes the same warning about greed, damage to our environment, and the lust for power. We fear these forces, but we do not fear them enough, he cautions.

So if we do not escape from pain, doubt, or suffering, what do fairy tales like Tolkien's offer an escape from? In his lecture, Tolkien argues that if people find themselves in prison and discover a way to break out and to escape to their real home, no one thinks this is a bad thing. In Tolkien's fiction, we escape from the narrow view that this world is all there is and from the declaration that life has no inherent meaning or purpose. His stories help free us from the futility and despair of our times and the notion that we can do little or nothing to change the world we live in.

Perhaps one of the most important aspects we find in Tolkien's fiction is an openness to possibility. This possibility is something that Bilbo learns to see through his adventure. As Tolkien declares in Bilbo's walking song found near the start of *The Fellowship of the Ring*, "Still round the corner there may wait a new road or a secret gate" (76). To readers who feel they are living in a closed world where all the doors and windows are shut and locked, Tolkien offers a key to escape the trap.

A third and final benefit that Tolkien outlines in his lecture "On Fairy-Stories" is *consolation*. He maintains that while these stories do not deny the existence of sorrow and failure, they also provide a "lifting of the heart" as well as a "fleeting glimpse of joy" that comes from "beyond the walls of the world" (153–54). In this sudden joyful turn—which Tolkien calls a *eucatastrophe*, the opposite of the catastrophe characteristic of tragedy—readers find not only consolation but faith and hope.

In a letter written to his son Christopher in 1944, Tolkien refers to the St. Andrews lecture and claims that fairy-stories provide this consolation because they give readers a "glimpse of truth" (*Letters*, 100). Tolkien uses an interesting metaphor for the realization that "this is how things really do work in the Great World for which our nature is made." He writes that we feel a sense of relief, as if one of our major limbs had been out of joint and then had suddenly snapped back. He concludes by stating that in *The Hobbit*, he knew he had written a story of worth when after rereading it some time after its publication, he had this exact experience of joy and relief.

On the final two pages of "On Fairy-Stories," in a section labeled "Epilogue," Tolkien makes a remarkable move for someone who was by nature reluctant to write much publically about issues of faith. "This 'joy' which I have selected as the mark of the true fairy-story . . . merits more consideration," he begins (155). Every subcreator, he maintains, hopes in his Secondary World to be drawing on an "underlying reality" of the Primary World. Thus—and here Tolkien makes his boldest claim—the joy any particular fairy-story produces may be seen as "a far-off gleam or echo" of the good news of the gospel story in the real world.

In the letter to Christopher mentioned above, Tolkien recalls that he concluded his lecture by saying that the Resurrection was "the greatest 'eucatastrophe' possible in the greatest Fairy Story" (*Letters*, 100). "Of course I do not mean that the Gospels tell what is *only* a fairy-story," Tolkien concludes. "But I do mean very strongly that they do tell a fairy-story: the greatest."

Verlyn Flieger and Douglas Anderson sum up Tolkien's conclusion in the epilogue this way:

> Consolation leads Tolkien to Joy, and Joy leads him to evangelium and the essay's Epilogue, a vision of *eucatastrophe* that occurs not in the imaginary world but in the real one. In calling the Gospels . . . the most successful fairy story . . . Tolkien is not making light of the Gospels, but revealing the underlying gravity and essential truth of fairy-stories. The little *eucatastrophes* of fairy-tales . . . are foreshadowings of the Great Tale. (14)

"In God's kingdom the presence of the greatest does not depress the small," Tolkien argues in the final paragraph of "On Fairy-Stories" (156). The good news of the Incarnation and the Resurrection "has not abrogated" the lesser fairy tales that man has made and continues to make. On the contrary, rather than doing away with our human fairy-stories, Tolkien concludes, "it has hallowed them."

An Indispensable Work

On October 2, 1937, readers opened *The Times Literary Supplement* to find a review written by C. S. Lewis about a remarkable new book. One "important truth" about this new book that Lewis points out is that it belongs to "a very small class" of books, the rare kind of book that "admits us to a world of its own—a world that seems to have been going on before we stumbled into it but which, once found by the right reader, becomes indispensable to him" ("Hobbit," 81). About this world found in *The Hobbit*, Lewis concludes: "You cannot anticipate it before you go there, as you cannot forget it once you have gone" (81).

A world that is indispensable. A world you cannot forget once you have been there. Tolkien fans know what Lewis was referring to. They know this world and agree that once found, it becomes an indispensable, unforgettable part of their lives.

They would also heartily agree with the author's own assessment of *The Hobbit*. In a letter written to Stanly Unwin on July 31, 1947, ten years after its publication, Tolkien observes: "*The Hobbit* was after all not as simple as it seemed" (*Letters*, 122).

The Hobbit is both a children's tale and something more. The Providence, purpose, and morality in *The Hobbit* go against the grain of the modern mind-set. In *The Hobbit*, Tolkien brings his readers into a world filled with meaning and purpose where they find stark contrasts between right and wrong. The same audience who might scoff at the Christian worldview in a different context find themselves embracing it in *The Hobbit*. Through his story, Tolkien is able—as his friend C. S. Lewis once described it—to "steal past those watchful dragons" ("Sometimes," 47). Readers who embrace the moral principles found in *The Hobbit*, and who long for a world like Middle-earth where these principles hold true, can find that place in the Christian faith its author professed.

And so as Bilbo hangs Sting up above his mantel, loans out his mithril coat to the museum at Michael Delving, and carefully packs away the cloak and hood lent to him by Dwalin on that first morning at the Green Dragon, we close the covers of *The Hobbit*. But just as Bilbo knows that he will need these precious items again, we, too, do not put *The Hobbit* on the top bookshelf but keep it close at hand, for we will want and need to return to it again and again.

After his grand birthday party in *The Fellowship of the Ring*, Bilbo sets out for one final adventure. He tells Gandalf that he hopes he can find a place where he can finish writing his memoirs—the story of his adventure with thirteen dwarves and a dragon named Smaug, which we saw him working on in the last chapter of *The Hobbit*.

Gandalf, using words in which we can hear Tolkien's doubts about his own creation, laughingly predicts, "Nobody will read the book, however it ends" (32).

"Oh, they may, in years to come," replies Bilbo.

And oh, they have.

And in the years still to come, they will continue to.

Reference List

Anderson, Douglas A. *The Annotated Hobbit.* Boston: Houghton Mifflin, 2002.

Auden, W. H. "The Hero Is a Hobbit." *New York Times,* October 31, 1954.

———. "The Quest Hero." In Zimbardo and Isaacs, *Understanding "The Lord of the Rings,"* 31–51.

Bramlett. Perry C. *I Am in Fact a Hobbit: An Introduction to the Life and Work of J. R. R. Tolkien.* Macon, GA: Mercer University Press, 2003.

Camus, Albert. "The Guest." In *Exile and the Kingdom,* 85–109. New York: Vintage, 1958.

Carpenter, Humphrey. *J. R. R. Tolkien: A Biography.* Boston: Houghton Mifflin, 2000.

Chesterton, G. K. *Orthodoxy.* New York: John Lane, 1908.

———. "The Red Angel." In *Tremendous Trifles,* 128–35. New York: Dodd, 1909.

Dickerson, Matthew T. *Following Gandalf: Epic Battles and Moral Victory in "The Lord of the Rings."* Grand Rapids: Brazos, 2003.

Duriez, Colin. *Tolkien and "The Lord of the Rings": A Guide to Middle-earth*. Mahwah, NJ: HiddenSpring, 2001.

Flieger, Verlyn, and Douglas A. Anderson. *Tolkien on Fairy-Stories*. London: HarperCollins, 2008.

Green, William H. *"The Hobbit": A Journey into Maturity*. New York: Twayne, 1995.

Grotta-Kurska, Daniel. *J. R. R. Tolkien: Architect of Middle Earth*. New York: Warner, 1976.

Huttar, Charles A. "Hell and the City: Tolkien and the Traditions of Western Literature." In Lobdell, *A Tolkien Compass*, 115–40.

Hibbs, Thomas. "Providence and the Dramatic Unity of *The Lord of the Rings*." In *"The Lord of the Rings" and Philosophy*, edited by Gregory Bassham and Eric Bronson, 167–78. Chicago: Open Court, 2003.

Jacobs, Alan. *The Narnian: The Life and Imagination of C. S. Lewis*. New York: HarperSanFrancisco, 2005.

Kilby, Clyde S. "Mythic and Christian Elements in Tolkien." In *Myth, Allegory, and Gospel*, edited by John Warwick Montgomery, 119–43. Minneapolis: Bethany Fellowship, 1974.

———. *Tolkien and "The Silmarillion."* Wheaton, IL: Harold Shaw, 1976.

Kocher, Paul H. *Master of Middle-Earth: The Fiction of J. R. R. Tolkien*. New York: Ballantine, 1977.

Lewis, C. S. *The Collected Letters of C. S. Lewis*. Vol. 3, *Narnia, Cambridge and Joy, 1950–1963*, edited by Walter Hooper. New York: HarperSanFrancisco, 2007.

———. "The Dethronement of Power." In Zimbardo and Isaacs, *Understanding "The Lord of the Rings*," 11–15.

———. "The Hobbit." In *On Stories and Other Essays on Literature*, 81–82.

———. *Letters to Malcolm: Chiefly on Prayer*. New York: Harvest, 1992.

———. *The Lion, the Witch and the Wardrobe*. New York: Harper Trophy, 1994.

———. *On Stories and Other Essays on Literature*. New Yotk: Harvest, 1982.

———. "On Three Ways of Writing for Children." In *On Stories and Other Essays on Literature*, 31–43.

———. *Prince Caspian*. New York: Harper Trophy, 1994.

———. *Reflections on the Psalms*. New York: Harvest, 1986.

———. *The Screwtape Letters*. New York: HarperOne, 1996.

———. *The Silver Chair*. New York: Harper Trophy, 1994.

———. "Sometimes Fairy Stories May Say Best What's to Be Said." In *On Stories and Other Essays on Literature*, 45–48.

———. *Surprised by Joy*. New York: Harvest, 1955.

———. "Tolkien's *The Lord of the Rings*." In *On Stories and Other Essays on Literature*, 83–90.

Lobdell, Jared, ed. *A Tolkien Compass*. Chicago: Open Court, 2003.

Manlove, Colin N. *Modern Fantasy: Five Studies*. Cambridge: Cambridge University Press, 1978.

Matthews, Dorothy. "The Psychological Journey of Bilbo Baggins." In Lobdell, *A Tolkien Compass*, 27–39.

Mills, David. "The Writer of Our Story: Divine Providence in *The Lord of the Rings*." *Touchstone* 15 (2002): 22–28.

Milton, John. *Paradise Lost*. London: Du Roveray, 1802.

Moorcock, Michael. "Epic Pooh." In *Arena 2: Anarchists in Fiction*, edited by Stuart Christie, 9–22. Oakland, CA: PM Press, 2011.

Moseley, Charles. *J. R. R. Tolkien*. Plymouth, England: Northcote House, 1997.

Pearce, Joseph. *Tolkien: Man and Myth*. New York: HarperCollins, 1999.

Pfotenhauer, Paul. "Christian Themes in Tolkien." *Cresset* 32 (January 1969): 13–15.

Purtill, Richard L. *Lord of the Elves and Eldils: Fantasy and Philosophy in C. S. Lewis and J. R. R. Tolkien*. San Francisco: Ignatius, 2006.

———. *J. R. R. Tolkien: Myth, Morality, and Religion*. San Francisco: Ignatius, 2003.

Rateliff, John D. *The History of The Hobbit; Part Two: Return to Bag-End.* Boston: Houghton Mifflin, 2007.

Rogers, Deborah, and Ivor Rogers. *J. R. R. Tolkien: A Critical Biography.* New York: Hippocrene, 1980.

Rogers, Jonathan. *The World According to Narnia: Christian Meaning in C. S. Lewis's Beloved Chronicles.* New York: Warner, 2005.

Rutledge, Fleming. *The Battle for Middle-earth: Tolkien's Divine Design in "The Lord of the Rings."* Grand Rapids: Eerdmans, 2004.

Shippey, Tom. "An Interview with Tom Shippey." In *The QPB Companion to "The Lord of the Rings,"* edited by Brandon Geist, 17–20. New York: Quality Paperback, 2001.

———. "C. S. Lewis." In *J. R. R. Tolkien Encyclopedia: Scholarship and Critical Assessment,* edited by Michael Drout, 356–60. New York: Routledge, 2006.

———. *The Road to Middle-earth: How J. R. R. Tolkien Created a New Mythology.* Boston: Houghton Mifflin, 2003.

Spacks, Patricia Meyer. "Power and Meaning in *The Lord of the Rings.*" In Zimbardo and Isaacs, *Understanding "The Lord of the Rings,"* 52–67.

Taylor, Daniel. *The Healing Power of Stories.* New York: Doubleday, 1996.

Tolkien, J. R. R. *The Fellowship of the Ring.* Boston: Houghton Mifflin, 1994.

———. "Foreword to the Second Edition." In *The Fellowship of the Ring*, xiii–xvi. Boston: Houghton Mifflin, 1994.

———. *The Hobbit*. Boston: Houghton Mifflin, 1994.

———. *The Letters of J. R. R. Tolkien*. Edited by Humphrey Carpenter. Boston: Houghton Mifflin, 2000.

———. "Mythopoeia." In *Tree and Leaf*, 97–98. Boston: Houghton Mifflin, 1989.

———. "On Fairy-Stories." In *The Monsters and the Critics: And Other Essays*, 109–61. New York: HarperCollins, 2006.

———. *The Return of the King*. Boston: Houghton Mifflin, 1994.

———. *The Two Towers*. Boston: Houghton Mifflin. 1994.

White, Michael. *Tolkien: A Biography*. New York: New American Library, 2001.

Zimbardo, Rose A., and Neil D. Isaacs, eds. *Understanding "The Lord of the Rings": The Best of Tolkien Criticism*. Boston: Houghton Mifflin, 2004.

About the Author

Devin Brown is a professor of English at Asbury University and is resident writer for Emblem Media. He is the author of *Not Exactly Normal, Inside Narnia, Inside Prince Caspian, Inside the Voyage of the Dawn Treader*, and this book, *The Christian World of "The Hobbit."*

Dr. Brown has spoken at many Lewis and Tolkien conferences in England and across the United States and has published numerous essays, book chapters, and inspirational articles on both these authors. In 2008, he served as Scholar-in-Residence at the Kilns, C. S. Lewis's home in Oxford. He lives in Lexington, Kentucky, with his wife, Sharon, and their fifteen-pound cat, Mr. Fluff.